VGM Careers for You

D0506420

CAREERS FOR

COURAGEOUS PEOPLE

& Other Adventurous Types

JAN GOLDBERG

SECOND EDITION

VGM Career Books

New York Chicago San Francisco Lisbon London Madrid Mexico City
Milan New Delhi San Juan Seoul Singapore Sydney Toronto

.54374452

The *McGraw-Hill* Companies

Library of Congress Cataloging-in-Publication Data

Goldberg, Jan
    Careers for courageous people & other adventurous types / by Jan
Goldberg. — 2nd ed.
      p. cm. — (VGM careers for you series)
      ISBN 0-07-143729-0 (alk. paper)
      1. Vocational guidance.   I. Title: Careers for courageous people and
other adventurous types.   II. Title: Courageous people & other adventurous
types.   III. Title.   IV. Series.

HF5382.G65   2004
331.702—dc22   2004002955

*This book is dedicated to the memory of
my parents, Sam and Sylvia Lefkovitz.*

1 2 3 4 5 6 7 8 9 0 DOC/DOC 3 2 1 0 9 8 7 6 5 4

ISBN 0-07-143729-0

McGraw-Hill books are available at special quantity discounts to use as premiums
and sales promotions, or for use in corporate training programs. For more
information, please write to the Director of Special Sales, Professional Publishing,
McGraw-Hill, Two Penn Plaza, New York, NY 10121-2298. Or contact your local
bookstore.

This book is printed on acid-free paper.

Contents

iii

Acknowledgments

The author gratefully acknowledges:

- The numerous professionals who graciously agreed to be profiled in this book.
- My dear husband, Larry, for his inspiration and vision.
- My children, Deborah, Bruce, and Sherri, for their encouragement and love.
- Family and close friends—Adrienne, Marty, Mindi, Cary, Michele, Paul, Michele, Alison, Steve, Marci, Steven, Brian, Jesse, Bertha, Aunt Estelle, Uncle Bernard, and Aunt Helen—for their faith and support.
- Diana Catlin, for her insights and input.

The editors also extend thanks to career writer Mark Rowh for his work in updating the 2005 edition of this book.

Preface

·····················

ere's a book for those of you who always thought you were a
bit more courageous or adventurous than your brothers, sisters, and friends. Inside you will find a wealth of information
about a number of occupations requiring an extra measure of
courage.

Want an inside look at some especially "adventurous" occupations? Then you'll no doubt be interested in the profiles sprinkled
throughout the book of real men and women engaged in such
careers. These profiles, many of which are told in the words of
their subjects, include a test pilot, a foreign correspondent, a Peace
Corps volunteer, a family of daredevils, a scuba diving instructor,
a hunting and fishing guide, a photojournalist, a skydiving
instructor, an FBI agent, an explosives handler, a police officer, and
a SWAT team member, among others. Although these career areas
do not represent an all-inclusive list by any means, they will give
you a sense of what it is like to engage in a courageous or adventurous career.

In addition, you'll find other information such as the type of
preparation needed for a given career area, the tasks performed
by those who hold jobs in the field, and sources of additional
information.

Chapter 1 looks at the nature of what we're calling "careers for
courageous people." This includes a look at various occupational
areas, some speculation about what is really involved in appealing
to one's adventurous spirit from an occupational viewpoint, and
some questions for you to answer about your prospects for pursuing such a career.

The second chapter covers some careers that might be pursued in faraway locations. Focusing on careers involving international travel, it covers the work of journalists who travel to cover the news, Peace Corps volunteers, missionaries, and others.

Chapter 3 looks at some of the careers of special interest to those who are active and physically fit. This includes careers as stunt performers, circus performers, bodyguards, Secret Service agents, cowboys or cowgirls, divers and diving instructors, test pilots, astronauts, sky divers, and river rafting guides.

The next chapter looks at some occupations for folks who enjoy the challenge of working with animals. Careers profiled here include beekeepers, animal trainers, zookeepers, and hunting and fishing guides.

Chapter 5 covers the world of law enforcement and some of the careers that constitute this career area. Information is provided on careers as uniformed police officers, sheriffs and deputy sheriffs, state police officers, detectives, guards, correctional officers, and more.

In Chapter 6, several other adventurous job areas are examined. This concluding chapter examines careers as firefighters, emergency medical technicians, private detectives and investigators, and more.

Addresses and websites for professional associations appear throughout the book. An appendix listing helpful books on career planning is also included.

Certainly, the occupations profiled in this book will not appeal to everyone. For some people, they may fall too far into the "risky" category. But for others, the careers profiled here might sound especially appealing.

Even for those with a particularly adventurous spirit, the career fields described throughout this book are offered as only some of the possibilities worth considering. You will be able to add more from your own experiences and those of friends and family or from further research. In the meantime, perhaps some of these overviews will inspire you in making your career plans.

CHAPTER ONE

Is the Adventurous Path Really for You?

Courage comes by being brave; fear comes by holding back.
—Publilius Syrus

Life shrinks or expands in proportion to one's courage.
—Anaïs Nin

Oh courage, oh yes! If only one had that, then life might be livable, in spite of everything.
—Henrik Ibsen

What does your mind conjure when you think of the adventures of the medieval King Arthur and the Knights of the Round Table? Do you picture swords, armor, villains, and damsels in distress? Do you recall heroic tales of valor, bravery, and good deeds?

While these well-known stories are not entirely true, they are not totally fictional either. History tells us that in the sixth century A.D. in Wales there lived a King Arthur who had a reputation for chivalry far beyond what was common in those days. Legend tells us that his Knights of the Round Table traveled the kingdom performing acts of courage and courtesy and that the handsomest, strongest, and bravest knight was, of course, Sir Lancelot. As Mary Macleod, in *The Book of King Arthur and His Knights*, tells it:

At the court of King Arthur were many valiant knights. I and some among them increased so in arms and worship that they surpassed all their fellows in prowess and noble deeds. But chief among them all was Sir Lancelot of the Lake, for in all tournaments and jousts and deeds of arms, both for life and death, he excelled all other knights, and never at any time was he overcome, unless it were by treason or enchantment.

Because of this, Queen Guinevere held him in higher favor than all other knights, and Sir Lancelot for his part loved the Queen above all other ladies and damsels all his life; and for her he did many deeds of arms, and more than once saved her from death by his noble chivalry.

Is the Courageous Path Right for You?

In contemporary times, too, some people dare to do things a little differently, to live perhaps "on the edge" and follow paths and careers that many might consider courageous or even dangerous. *Merriam-Webster's Collegiate Dictionary* defines *courage* as "mental or moral strength to venture, persevere, and withstand danger, fear, or difficulty."

Are you the kind of person who admires Sir Lancelot and who is drawn to following a similar path—not necessarily saving damsels in distress, but living a life that others might consider adventurous or courageous? Do friends and acquaintances tell you they think you are courageous? Are you a risk taker? Do you like to move away from the mundane into perhaps less secure behavior and practices? Take the following quiz, answering yes or no to each question. You may discover you are courageous, and one of the careers profiled within this book might be just perfect for you!

SELF-TEST

1. Do I get bored easily by doing things that are routine?
2. Am I willing to take risks to make gains I feel are important?
3. Do I enjoy living on the edge?
4. Do I avoid playing it safe?
5. Do I think of situations being challenging rather than dangerous?
6. Am I willing to enlarge my comfort zone and try new things?
7. Do I feel physically and mentally strong?

If you're truly a courageous type, your answer to some or all of these questions will be an affirmative one. After all, such people generally exhibit most of the traits listed below.

SOME TRAITS OF COURAGEOUS PEOPLE

- Impatience with mundane schedules and routines
- High levels of curiosity
- A strong preference for firsthand experience over watching from afar
- The willingness to take risks when it will lead to a desired result
- The ability to act without undue worry about consequences
- A passion for physical activity
- A liking for activities that produce physical or emotional thrills
- A disdain for always taking the easiest path
- A positive outlook
- The ability to solve problems
- A strong interest in acquiring new information or enjoying new experiences

- Physical strength, agility, and endurance
- Mental toughness

Courage, Careers, and You

If you're the courageous type, perhaps you can find an outlet for your interests through hobbies or sports, such as mountain climbing, kayaking, or big-game hunting. But that may not be enough.

A more fulfilling approach might be to consider occupations that appeal to the adventurous side of human nature. Just what constitutes an adventure? If you ask different people, you'll get a variety of opinions.

To some, adventure equates with risk. At one extreme, this means facing physical danger. Climbing Mount Everest, flying combat aircraft, or sailing alone across the Pacific are just a few examples of this type of adventure.

In another direction, risk might simply refer to the possibility of failure, or perhaps simply to the potential for embarrassment or disappointment. Performing in a play in front of hundreds of people, learning to ice skate, or taking an oral exam to earn an advanced degree might be considered, in this light, to be adventurous.

Certainly, a common element of adventure is a sense of excitement. During an adventurous activity, and often in anticipating it, feelings of excitement are the norm. But of course, different people may have vastly different ideas of what an "exciting" activity is.

For example, consider the world of auto racing. For some, the chance to work in this field may be the ultimate adventure. At the most visible this would mean working as a driver, but other similar roles may also prove exciting. For some people, serving as a crew chief or mechanic for a NASCAR racing team might be considered nearly as adventurous as working as a driver.

Dozens more examples could also be cited, but the main point is that there is no uniform definition of adventure, at least when it comes to careers.

Certainly, all too many occupations offer little or no sense of excitement. This is not to say they aren't perfectly respectable jobs, but few people would label them as adventurous by any stretch of the imagination. For example, it's hard to imagine that anyone would consider working on an assembly line (or working as a drafter or sales clerk or purchasing agent) as being an example of a career requiring a special measure of courage.

On the other hand, some careers involve physical danger or other genuine risks. Of course living itself is dangerous, and almost any action involves some measure of risk. For example, if you spend sixty minutes a day driving on a crowded freeway to commute to your job as an accountant, there is always the chance that you will be involved in an automobile accident. But describing your accounting career as dangerous would be a real stretch.

Conversely, if you work as a test pilot, flying experimental aircraft on a routine basis, the element of danger is constantly at hand. The same is true for other careers involving honest-to-goodness physical danger (working as a Navy SEAL or a bomb demolition expert or an astronaut, just to name a few). Few would argue that these and other such occupations can justifiably be considered adventurous, or that the people who pursue them might be regarded as courageous.

The same can be said of careers involving travel to faraway places. In the centuries before supersonic travel and instantaneous communication, one classic example of the adventurer was the traveler who explored faraway lands. Long distance travel is far more common today, however, and what was once considered exotic or glamorous may now fall within the realm of routine business or personal activity, at least for some. But for most people, working in jobs that take them to faraway locations still falls within the aegis of adventurous activity. For example, an

American journalist who covers conflicts in Afghanistan, Iraq, or elsewhere certainly requires a good measure of courage. Similarly, jobs that involve working with exotic animals, confronting dangerous criminals, or facing other types of risks may be set apart from a host of other careers.

In this book, the emphasis is on careers that involve, at least potentially, some degree of physical danger. Certainly this varies not only among occupations, but from one situation to the next. For example, most people would include police officers in the "courageous" category, but in reality their experiences run the gamut from the adventurous to the mundane. An undercover police officer or a SWAT team member, for example, would have a vastly different experience from an officer who performs purely administrative or clerical tasks.

Perhaps the most important factor to consider is that only you can decide the full definition of *courageous*, at least as it applies to you. If you're the type who yearns for an occupational experience in this direction, then any efforts to explore some of the more adventurous career possibilities will be worth your time.

CHAPTER TWO

Careers in Faraway Places

Courage is doing what you're afraid to do.
There can be no courage unless you're scared.
—Eddie Rickenbacker

Only a generation or two ago, traveling outside North America was a privilege enjoyed by a relatively small number of people. But in the twenty-first century, the nations of the world are connected in ways few would have imagined. The development of multinational corporations, affordable air travel, and online communications has rendered the world a smaller place. At the same time, the growth of international trade and travel has meant that more and more opportunities can be found for living and working in other countries.

The expansion of international opportunities has been a boon for those for whom the lure of faraway places is too much to resist. For those whose yearnings include a "home away from home" in which to live and work, the following possibilities offer potential.

Foreign Correspondents

When a war breaks out in the Middle East or some other point far from the United States and Canada, how do we know about it? Today we can obtain news from a variety of sources, but none are more important than the journalists who travel to other nations with the specific purpose of covering newsworthy events. These journalists, traditionally known as foreign correspondents, are employed by networks, news services, television or radio stations, and major magazines or newspapers. They may also operate as freelance agents. Their responsibilities include monitoring trends and events in other countries, gathering news of possible interest, and reporting it to North American audiences.

Zeroing in on What a Foreign Correspondent Does

Acting as reporters, foreign correspondents travel to various countries where they are responsible for tracking down and uncovering information via news conferences, research, private sources, wire services, interviews, and any other means they can devise. They then must organize the information and produce articles that are clear, concise, and well written for their audiences in the United States, Canada, or whatever their home country is. Since newsworthy events may occur at any time, being a foreign correspondent is hardly a nine-to-five job. And since many newsworthy events are also dangerous, this ingredient may also be part of the job.

When working overseas, journalists may cover any number of stories. Those that tend to be most visible, such as wars and disasters, may overshadow the many other stories that may be of interest to domestic audiences, from political developments to cultural trends. Of course the former bring journalists closer to danger, and in that way are definitely at the high end of the adventure spectrum. But simply traveling to and living in other countries, not to mention covering newsworthy events there, provides its own form of adventure.

In covering stories, reporters investigate leads, examine documents, observe events in person, and interview sources. Along with taking notes, they may take photographs or shoot videos. Some work is performed in the field, often with the use of notebook computers or portable video equipment, while other stories may be completed or edited in an office environment. Print journalists (those who write for newspapers and magazines) work somewhat differently from those who prepare television segments or radio reports, but they also have much in common. Some also work with more than one type of media. A television reporter, for example, may also write books about his or her experiences.

Some journalists risk their lives while covering wars or other tumultuous events. Ernie Pyle, a popular reporter who was killed in World War II, may be the most well-known victim of this type, but he is far from the only one. In every war, reporters are among the casualties. Typically they volunteer for hazardous duty, and it is important to realize that not all journalists assigned to cover the news in other countries face such danger. At the same time, this is a path that may attract those who are especially daring.

The role of journalists in the 2003 invasion of Iraq by the United States and several of its allies may be typical of what is expected of many foreign correspondents. They faced the challenge of analyzing a complex situation and providing meaningful information for a public hungry for up-to-date details, all within the framework of a dangerous situation. Some enhanced their reputations and made substantial career progress. A few, unfortunately, became the object of news coverage themselves, as they suffered injuries or death.

These journalists realize that some element of danger is an unavoidable part of their jobs. Those covering not just wars, but also other types of situations, do so with the understanding that working in this field can be dangerous. Political uprisings, outbreaks of disease, fires, floods, and similar events also pose hazards for reporters covering the international scene.

Qualifications and Training Required for Foreign Correspondents

You can expect serious competition for foreign correspondent positions. Typically, only reporters with extensive experience will be given the opportunity to serve as foreign correspondents. In general, employers seek candidates who have earned degrees in journalism or broadcast communications—or possibly in liberal arts with a strong background and experience in journalism. Outstanding written and oral communication skills, a "nose for news," an ability to handle difficult situations, curiosity, research and word processing skills, persistence, patience, fortitude, honesty, and good people skills are some desirable qualities.

Those who are considering this kind of work should focus on classes in political science, world history, law, economics, psychology, foreign languages, English, journalism, sociology, and communications. Practical experience through school newspapers, yearbooks, local newspapers, and internships are invaluable.

Salaries for Foreign Correspondents

Depending on the employer, the location, and the correspondent's previous experience, salaries can range from $25,000 to $85,000 or more.

Meet a Foreign Correspondent

Jerry King did not intend to become a foreign correspondent, planning instead to work as a teacher. But after enrolling at a university in Canada, he became involved in sports broadcasting. One job led to another, including spots as a radio deejay in Bermuda and a radio journalist in England, followed by a position as a television correspondent in Germany.

"As a foreign correspondent, you have to be able to function in a variety of circumstances," he said. "During my career I've been in Northern Ireland, Vietnam, Lebanon, Afghanistan, Somalia, Iran, Iraq—the list goes on and on. In these situations, you have to exist without the creature comforts of home and also be creative and quick thinking."

According to King, foreign correspondents often rely on journalists who live and work in the area. When he was working in Germany, for example, he obtained much of his information through local reporters. When possible he would go back and get a particular slant or ask some specific questions, but his original information often came from other journalists. An exception was when a breaking story occurred (such as an airplane hijacking), where he could observe firsthand what was happening.

"I was lucky," he said. "In Poland I had a translator who knew Lech Walesa personally, so we had more access to him than some of the other journalists. I also had a cameraman in Lebanon who, on Christmas day, went around taking cookies to all the gunmen in the front lines because he wanted to make them his friends. He once told me that if you are caught someplace with a group of 'bad people,' you should always shake hands and keep shaking hands because they don't like to shoot you when they're shaking hands."

On one assignment, King was the first network television correspondent to come out of Warsaw after martial law was declared. He and other journalists had been largely cut off from outside contact, and they thought the world had lost interest in the story because the situation had not changed much. But when he was suddenly able to make his way out of the country by train, he was amazed at how much interest there actually was. He returned to the United States quickly, and the next day he appeared on several network television shows.

"I've seen humanity at its best and at its worst," King said. "As a foreign correspondent, you are allowed to meet some pretty interesting people and witness some really fascinating things." He added that there is sometimes a "boredom factor" when journalists are prevented from doing anything but wait, and that many times the job involves long hours in researching, interviewing, writing, and rewriting stories. King noted that these factors are offset, though, by the fact that the job can be truly enjoyable.

For Additional Information

Dow Jones Newspaper Fund
P.O. Box 300
Princeton, NJ 08543
http://djnewspaperfund.dowjones.com

National Association of Broadcasters
1771 N Street NW
Washington, DC 20036
www.nab.org

Newspaper Association of America
1921 Gallows Road, Suite 600
Vienna, VA 22182
www.naa.org

Radio and Television News Directors Foundation
1600 K Street NW, Suite 700
Washington, DC 20006
www.rtndf.org

Peace Corps Volunteers

In 1961, at a time when the cold war between East and West raged and Germany stood divided, President John F. Kennedy launched the Peace Corps. In the decades since then, Peace Corps volunteers have maintained the same mission: providing support to battle disease, poverty, hunger, and deprivation all over the globe and to teach people of other nations about America and Americans in order to promote world understanding.

More than 170,000 Americans have served as Peace Corps volunteers in 136 nations. Today, volunteers are performing their services in countries in Asia, the Middle East, South and Central America, the Caribbean, the Pacific, Africa, and Europe.

Most participants are under thirty (with a median age of twenty-five), but six percent of all volunteers are over fifty, and men and women in their seventies and eighties have participated.

Zeroing in on What a Peace Corps Volunteer Does

Peace Corps assignments originate when host countries make specific requests for individuals with particular expertise. Some of the skills most often requested fall in the areas of technical education, primary and secondary education, health and nutrition, natural resources, and agriculture. Volunteers are not asked simply to go over to these countries and do all the work. Their role is to bring the necessary information, techniques, and expertise to the host country citizens so that they may perform these tasks on their own.

Qualifications and Training Required for Peace Corps Volunteers

Applicants for the Peace Corps must be United States citizens who are at least eighteen years old (no limit on the upper end) and healthy, out of financial debt, and willing to undergo an eight- to twelve-week training program and a two-year service period. Additionally, workshops are held to reinforce skills and formulate and disseminate plans.

Married couples without children are eligible as long as they meet all qualifications. It usually takes about ten months from the receipt of an assignment to the beginning of training. While applicants are able to indicate a preference for a geographic area or areas, this limits possibilities for placement.

Most assignments require a minimum of a bachelor's degree. In some cases an associate degree may suffice. Some jobs require a master's degree or three to five years of experience in lieu of, or in addition to, a college degree.

Volunteers receive transportation to and from their assignment locations and twenty-four days of vacation each year. Free medical and dental care is provided along with a monthly stipend to allow for housing, food, clothes, and other living expenses. Student loan payments may be deferred for the time period of Peace Corps service. Upon fulfilling this commitment, volunteers are given a readjustment allowance in addition to being aided in their job search. Some opt to take advantage of the available eligibility for federal employment on a noncompetitive basis. Also, many colleges and universities offer special scholarships and assistantships for volunteers who return home.

Returning volunteers cite the following benefits of Peace Corps service: a way to see diverse parts of the world, an opportunity to get to know and be of help to people in Third World countries, a rewarding feeling, and in many cases substantial personal growth.

Meet a Peace Corps Volunteer

Kathleen Klug learned about the Peace Corps through social studies classes in high school. Even before college, she began to develop an interest in other cultures and community service—interests that can be readily pursued in the Peace Corps.

"I attended Peace Corps recruiting presentations at my university to obtain more specific information about becoming a volunteer," she said. "In the fall of my senior year, I submitted the lengthy Peace Corps application and interviewed with a recruiter."

Klug found that speaking with the recruiter gave her a clearer picture of the application process. She was told that it probably would be difficult to find her a placement due to her nontechnical background. Over the years, the Peace Corps has preferred to recruit individuals who have degrees or backgrounds in subjects such as medicine, farming, horticulture, engineering, construction, physics, chemistry, math, and teaching English as a second language. However, others may also be accepted. In Klug's case, some of her course work and volunteer experience helped her to pass this initial stage of the application process. She graduated with a B.S. in psychology and political science and also had completed CPR/first aid certification and some health education course work.

After her interview, she kept in regular contact with her recruiter and waited three to four months until she received a nomination in the health nutrition extension. At that time, she needed to complete information for a background check, including fingerprinting, and have a complete medical exam. Eventually she received an invitation to serve as water sanitation health educator in Ghana, West Africa.

"The whole process took about eight months from the time I applied until the time I left for Ghana," Klug recalled. "I knew some individuals who, either because of luck or a technical background, completed the entire process in one month." She explained that the recruiting process may boil down to a certain country needing a particular type of skilled volunteer and a Peace Corps applicant having those skills and being available at that time.

Before leaving the United States, Klug completed preliminary training with other trainees going to Ghana. The participants in her training group were in their twenties and thirties, for the most part, and came from all over the United States. This provided a time for people to get to know one another, gain general information about the Peace Corps, and learn about Ghana. Then Klug and about fifty other trainees traveled to Ghana for a ten-week training session. This included training in language, culture, and technical education in addition to field experience.

She was then assigned to a site in the Kumasi region of the country in a medium-size village called Manso Nkwanta, which was the district capital. During the first few months, she spent most of her time meeting with people in the village and surrounding district villages and evaluating the water sanitation health education needs.

As a health educator she reported to the fifteen-person Manso Nkwanta District Health and Sanitation Committee, the Ministry of Community Development district officer, the district coordinator of the Ghana National Commission on Children, and three district health nurses.

One of her most important accomplishments was to help organize a project committee for the construction of a ten-seat Kumasi Ventilated Improved Pit (KVIP) latrine in Manso Nkwanta. In working with the traditional village council, communal labor was organized to construct the latrine. The construction was complemented by a health education seminar on sanitation.

She also worked with the community development district officer to initiate health and sanitation education and awareness in the district through presentations and informal discussions, and spent time at the district clinic assisting the community health nurses with record keeping, baby weighing, immunizations, and nutritional counseling. Her work also included teaching English at a local school as a secondary service project along with her role in water and sanitation health education.

"During my service, I enjoyed traveling to other regions of Ghana as well as to surrounding countries," Klug said. "Another factor that made my Peace Corps experience interesting was that I lived with the royal family in my village." Since ceremonies such as the swearing-in of a chief often took place in the traditional district capital, Manso Nkwanta, she was able to attend most of these events.

"The best advice I can give to a potential United States Peace Corps volunteer is to be patient and flexible during the whole process," she said. "Some individuals have very specific expectations, and those are generally the people who quit prior to their close of service." But those who, like Klug, maintain the right attitude, often echo the recruitment slogan you may have heard about the Peace Corps: "The toughest job you'll ever love."

For Additional Information

National Peace Corps Association
1900 L Street NW, Suite 205
Washington, DC 20036
www.rpcv.org

Peace Corps
1990 K Street NW, Room 9320
Washington, DC 20526
www.peacecorps.gov

AmeriCorps Volunteer

If the Peace Corps sounds interesting but you'd rather explore the far corners of this country than take off for other nations, consider the domestic programs known collectively as AmeriCorps. These public service programs provide opportunities within the United States in areas such as education, public safety, health, and the environment. More than 250,000 men and women have served in AmeriCorps since 1994, performing tasks such as tutoring children, building affordable housing, cleaning parks and streams, teaching computer skills, and helping communities respond to disasters.

Some AmeriCorps programs address local needs, while others operate on a national basis. Of special interest to younger Americans is AmeriCorps NCCC, which is a ten-month, full-time residential program for men and women between the ages of eighteen and twenty-four. Members serve in teams based at one of five campuses across the country, from which they are sent to perform public service in any of several surrounding states.

In addition to a modest monthly salary, AmeriCorps members are eligible to receive an education award that can be used for college tuition or related costs, or to repay student loans.

For more information, check out the AmeriCorps website at www.americorps.gov.

Missionaries

Missionaries have been a part of the religious world for thousands of years. Christians, Buddhists, Muslims, and others have sent missionaries to teach people about their religions and to attract new followers.

The work of missionaries has been a central part of the history of Christianity. In the early days of the Christian church, missionaries helped spread the tenets of the new religion through-out the Roman Empire. After Christianity became dominant in Europe, missionaries from various nations continued to travel to other lands to take the teachings of the church to new believers. After the Protestant Revolution, this included not just the Catholic Church, but various denominations that developed their own beliefs about the importance of missionary work and the ways in which it should be carried out.

During the colonization of North America and many other regions of the world, Christian missionaries played key roles. The Spanish, for example, established numerous missions throughout the New World, and the British and French also sent missionaries to convert native peoples to Christianity.

The United States also has a strong heritage of missionary activity. Some of this has taken place within the country itself, for missionary work is not restricted to outreach to other countries. At the same time, a major emphasis of such work has always been directed at other nations, a trend that continues to the present. Today, thousands of men and women from the United States and Canada serve as missionaries in Africa, Asia, and other parts of the world.

Zeroing in on What a Missionary Does

Just what do missionaries do? That depends on both their individual backgrounds and the priorities of the organizations that sponsor them. Many missionaries are ordained clergy, and their roles focus on functions such as leading worship services and conducting baptisms or other religious rites.

Other missionaries act in a lay capacity, meaning they are not ordained but are still working on behalf of a church or other religious organization. Both lay missionaries and those who are ordained may also take on a wide range of other tasks such as building schools, providing medical care, teaching, or helping farmers improve agricultural methods.

In some cases, a primary goal of missionaries is to bring new believers into their faith. In others, the objective is not necessarily to convert people, but merely to serve their needs in a way that demonstrates kindness and concern for one's fellow human beings.

In 1871 the search for one of the most famous missionaries of all time culminated with the words, "Dr. Livingstone, I presume." The phrase was addressed to David Livingstone, a Scottish medical missionary and explorer; the words were spoken by Henry M. Stanley, a journalist employed by London and New York newspapers. Living mostly in the Zambesi area of Africa, Livingstone had lost touch with the outside world until Stanley found him. The interesting nature of this story later sparked both written and visual chronicles of the event and the adventures of Stanley and Livingstone.

Typically, we think of missionaries as religious individuals who set out to spread the word about their religion and attempt to win followers. But it is not only for religious purposes that missionaries travel all across the globe; they also go to foreign lands to help the large numbers of people who live in the less-developed countries in the world.

Missionaries may find themselves in the jungles of South America, in the mountains of Asia, or the "back country" of Africa—or even in some cities in the United States. They live and work with the local people, trying to help them initiate and maintain improvements in their lives and their standard of living.

Conditions may vary a great deal from one mission to the next, depending on the missionary's assigned tasks and the area to which he or she has been assigned. Some areas of the world are still quite primitive, and since missionaries live as the natives do, whether in New York City or a tiny village in Africa, they may also be living with few amenities. Danger is often an element of everyday life. Also, understandably, the pace of life in a remote area is likely to be slower and less complicated than city life in America or Europe. However, missionaries may take part in retreats, camping trips, and seminars and become hosts to other visiting missionaries or members of their home church. Mission activities may include participation in sports, films, books, and musical groups such as choirs.

Following are some categories of missionaries:

- **Evangelists** are religious leaders who quote and read from the Bible and explain their own life stories in an attempt to convince others of the value of deep religious faith. Evangelists may travel from house to house, speak before large groups, or address audiences via television, radio, or the Internet.
- **Mission clergy** act as congregational pastors, preaching sermons and leading prayer services. When necessary, they visit the sick and those in need.
- **Church planners** serve as leaders of the church who assemble parishioners in a particular place, helping to set up a religious congregation.
- **Farm experts** help put irrigation systems into place and share information necessary to control pests and diseases.
- **Home economists** teach the fundamentals of cooking, sewing, and preserving food.
- **Mission teachers** are expected to provide the fundamentals of learning for the children of the mission staff as well as the local children and adults. Both religious education and improved methods of living are stressed. This usually includes teaching reading and writing and may include translating the Bible into local languages.
- **Nonordained workers** (lay mission workers) usually perform the same jobs they would carry out in their home environment.
- **Skilled workers** such as carpenters, photographers, or nurse's aides, for example, go to a specific place for a specified period of time for the purpose of sharing their

particular expertise. Those with varying skills are called upon to be of service as doctors, nurses, farm experts, pilots, teachers, religious leaders, social workers, and so on.

Qualifications and Training Required for Missionaries

Dedicated courageous spirits who are interested in becoming missionaries should begin their quest at the high school level by joining school or religious programs, working with those who are less fortunate, acting as camp counselors, volunteering in big sister or big brother programs, or participating in any other organized group activity that focuses on helping others. Teenagers should begin to make inquiries about missionary work through their church or a recruiting agency.

Most commonly, career missionaries obtain college degrees from church-supported colleges or Bible schools. Often missionaries have an additional three years of seminary experience during which they study theology, educational psychology, church history, approaches to teaching, and the Bible. Some missionaries are ordained priests or ministers. However, additional technical skills or areas of expertise are looked upon with favor.

Upon completion of formal schooling, most missionaries spend time in an apprenticed position working with veteran missionaries. During this time, they gain a firsthand knowledge and understanding of the culture and language of their host countries.

Some colleges allow students to serve as interns—an experience that allows them to find out what it is like, more or less, to be a missionary. DePauw University, for example, offers students the opportunity to spend one month as missionaries. During past years, students have assisted Guatemalans caught in earthquakes, helped to bring electricity to a small Peruvian village, and were involved in many other positive deeds in diverse areas of the world.

Personal characteristics that are desirable for those wishing to pursue missionary work include the ability to be independent, the desire to make a difference in the world by helping people, the ability to adapt to surroundings no matter how difficult they are, the facility to learn a new language quickly, the knack of being a team player, and the skill to assess situations quickly and act upon them as necessary. Other positive attributes include patience, fortitude, and empathy. Since missionaries are often on call twenty-four hours a day, it is important to be physically and mentally strong. Last, but certainly not least, a positive disposition and a sense of humor are great assets.

Though advancement is usually not a priority, it is possible to work up to serving on a mission board or heading a large mission and supervising a number of other missionaries.

Sometimes the pattern of life that has been set for missionaries doesn't end when they return home or complete their initial term of service. Individuals often continue their support of missionary projects by working to raise money and in other ways serving their churches and other community organizations. Some end up dedicating their whole lives to helping others.

One outstanding example was Mother Teresa, an Albanian-born Roman Catholic missionary. Her tireless efforts on behalf of the sick and the poor in India are legendary. In 1950 she established the Missionaries of Charity, a group of Roman Catholic sisters. In 1979, she won the Nobel Peace Prize. She was considered a rare humanitarian, and her wisdom and pathos are evidenced in her words:

> *Even the rich are hungry for love, for being cared for, for being wanted, for having someone to call their own. There must be a reason why some people can afford to live well. They must have worked for it. I only feel angry when I see waste. When I see people throwing away things that we could use. The biggest disease today is not leprosy or tuberculosis, but rather the feeling of being unwanted.*

For Additional Information

American Ministries
P.O. Box 3737
Arlington, VA 22203
www.americanministries.com

American Missionary Fellowship
P.O. Box 37
Villanova, PA 19085
www.americanmissionary.org

Christian Missionary Fellowship International
P.O. Box 501020
Indianapolis, IN 46250
www.cmfi.org

Evangelical Lutheran Church in America
8765 West Higgins Road
Chicago, IL 60631
www.elca.org

Intercristo
19303 Fremont Avenue North
Seattle, WA 98133
www.jobleads.org

InterAct Ministries
31000 Southeast Kelso Road
Boring, OR 97009
www.interactministries.org

Presbyterian Church in America
1700 North Brown Road
Lawrenceville, GA 30043
www.pcanet.org

CHAPTER THREE

Careers for the Strong and Agile

Fall seven times, stand up eight.
—Japanese proverb

Staying in shape is (or should be) important to everyone. But it is particularly vital to those who use personal strength and agility in their occupations every day. For example, consider the work done by specialists who perform stunts in the film industry. Tasks such as simulating a fistfight, climbing a cliff, or falling from a roof without getting hurt definitely require a substantial measure of physicality. The same is true of a number of occupational areas. This chapter takes a look at several such careers.

Stunt Performers

Stunt performers have existed since the early years of motion pictures. Frank Hanaway, believed to be the very first stunt performer, appeared in the 1903 film *The Great Train Robbery*. The first stuntwoman appearing in a motion picture was Helen Bigson, who began her career in the 1914 film series *The Hazards of Helen*. Overwhelmingly, however, stunt performers have been men. Because an injury to a star could end production on a film, television, or stage production, stunt performers became important, particularly to the movie industry. Chances are, no matter how "macho" your favorite star is, a stuntman or stunt-woman performs his or her stunts.

Stunt performers can be seen in car crashes, on horseback, falling from buildings, leaping from speeding automobiles, bouncing off the tops of airplanes, and engaging in fights with man and beast. The James Bond movies (and many others) owe much of their popularity to the incredible stunts that have become a trademark of these films.

Zeroing in on What a Stunt Performer Does

Stunt roles are usually divided into either "double" or "nonde-script." The first refers to instances when the stunt performer acts as if he or she were the star actor and "doubles" for the star. A "nondescript" role usually involves a lesser character who has a dangerous scene. For example, a driver in a highway chase scene could be a "nondescript" role.

Screenwriters are usually the ones who decide when a stunt, known to add excitement to a movie, will be included. But once stunts are written into the script, it is the director who makes the decisions regarding how the stunt will be orchestrated and what it will look like in its final form. Often stunt coordinators work with directors to determine the best and safest way to incorporate the stunt into the scene. Though a stunt often lasts only a few seconds, setting it up can take many long hours. Stunt performers work along with other departments such as makeup, prop, set design, wardrobe, and special effects. Camera angles must be coordinated with everything else so that, with luck, the stunt may be recorded in only one take.

Though stunt performers are courageous, they keep danger to a minimum whenever possible. For instance, in carrying out stunts involving entering a building that is on fire, the performer wears fireproof clothing and applies a protective cream to the skin. Going a step further, stunt performers often build protective equipment of their own design.

Since stunt professionals are expected to bring their own protective items, such as spine protectors, burning suits, special boots, and knee pads, they have to absorb the costs of this equipment. More elaborate equipment, such as safety nets, ramps, breathing equipment, air bags, and special pulleys and rigging, are usually rented by the stunt coordinator.

Sometimes directors call upon stunt troupes, which are loose business associations of stunt men and women who can professionally handle virtually any kind of stunt.

Qualifications and Training Required for Stunt Performers

Individuals usually begin as extras and move into stunting as their abilities strengthen. By checking in every day, they learn when extras will be hired. Those new to the field usually begin with relatively simple roles, such as one of twenty people involved in a brawl. Initially, they probably only work for an hour or two at a time.

Many stunt performers are children of established professionals. Stunt careers begin at ages as young as eighteen and may extend beyond the age of sixty.

Though a number of stunt schools do exist, most stunt performers learn their skills by working alongside more experienced stunt performers for several years. While there are no specific educational requirements, many stunt professionals have college degrees. Knowledge of all aspects of filmmaking is desirable so that performers can effectively design safe stunts and equipment. Schools and short courses offered in Hollywood teach analytical skills necessary to pull off certain stunts. It is important that stunt professionals know how to make calculations such as rates of falling, effects of weight or impact, and angles of departure for jumps.

Since athletic ability is necessary to be successful as a stunt performer, many are former high school or college athletes. Some are even world or Olympic champions. Many stunt professionals have backgrounds in ballet, race driving, gymnastics, acrobatics, or weight lifting. A number of former rodeo riders and football players are now doing stunt work.

If you are interested in pursuing this kind of work, study movies and television, develop physical strength and coordination, and learn to fall, ride, and climb. Stunt coordinators need five to ten years of experience before they can act in this capacity.

Job Settings and Salaries for Stunt Performers

Competition for stunt work is fierce, but the best opportunities tend to exist in California, which still serves as the heart of the film industry. Jobs can also be found in other states where motion pictures are made, including New York, Arizona, Texas, and Florida.

The top ten Hollywood stunt professionals are undeniably well paid. Some earn more than $250,000 per year. The next one hundred or so make in the neighborhood of $100,000 per year. The majority of stunt performers are paid the Screen Actors Guild rate plus a "stunt adjustment" based on the danger of the stunt involved. Usually that's for performing the stunt once; if you do it again, you get paid that rate once more. A stunt performer once earned $150,000 for jumping off an eleven-hundred-foot tower in Toronto and waiting until he was only about three hundred feet off the ground to release his parachute. However, sums like this are rare. In fact, only a small number of individuals are able to support themselves with full-time work as stunt professionals. The best stunt coordinators, few though they are, make as much as $400,000.

Usually stunt professionals are covered by medical and disability insurance that the film company provides while they are working. Additionally, they are covered by workers' compensation.

Regardless of the inherent drawbacks in this job, a large number of people are interested in this career because of the competitive challenge, the thrill, and the opportunity to work in motion pictures.

For Additional Information

Screen Actors Guild
5757 Wilshire Boulevard
Los Angeles, CA 90036
www.sag.org

Stuntmen's Association of Motion Pictures
10660 Riverside Drive, Second Floor, Suite E
Toluca Lake, CA 91602
www.stuntmen.com

Circus Performers

Circuses have long been a source of entertainment. In ancient Rome, performances involving wild animals, chariot races, and demonstrations of athleticism thrilled crowds of thousands. In the eighteenth and nineteenth centuries, circuses in Europe and America became especially prominent, bringing a touch of the exotic to both rural and urban audiences.

In recent years, the popularity of circuses has declined somewhat. Once, the arrival of a circus in town was considered by many to be an exciting and routine-breaking event since other types of entertainment were less common. Today, on the other hand, circuses must compete with professional sporting events, theatrical performances, rock and country music concerts, movies, and other widely available forms of entertainment.

Despite competition for the attention of potential audiences, there is still a place for circuses and the performers and other employees who operate them. In fact, some circuses, such as the Cirque du Soleil, have gained new levels of popularity.

People go to the circus to enjoy acts that are entertaining, daring, or funny. As advertised, circuses try to provide "the most stupendous, the most colossal, and the most sensational" acts. You'll find these performances at country fairs, rodeos, ice and water shows, state fairs, amusement parks, and carnivals, among other places of interest.

A two-hour circus performance usually consists of approximately forty acts. Though each act may only last about five minutes, many hours have been put into polishing the act.

Zeroing in on What a Circus Performer Does

A circus begins with all circus performers taking part in an opening parade, dressed in elaborate costumes that the circus (not the individual) owns. Some performers work alone and some work together in groups called troupes. Single performers include unicycle riders, tightrope walkers, jugglers, and high stilt walkers. Trapeze artists, balancing acts, dancers, human cannonballs, living statues, musicians, and teeterboard dancers depend on several people working together. Animal trainers may work alone or with other trainers.

Since a circus may perform in fifty towns or more in one year, circus performers do a great deal of traveling. Time spent at any one place may range from a couple of days to two or three months. Performances may take place two or even three times per day. In between, circus performers take care of their costumes, practice, apply makeup, gather and set up whatever equipment is needed, and perform any other tasks required of them by the circus management. You can be sure they are kept very busy.

Qualifications and Training Required for Circus Performers

There are no specific educational requirements for circus performers, but in most cases, a considerable amount of training is necessary. Virtually all who have a place in the circus have worked for years to perfect their acts. They have gone through the exercise and training necessary to allow their bodies to be in top shape.

Between 75 and 80 percent of circus performers come from circus families. One such group is the Nocks family.

Meet a Family of Circus Performers

The Nockses are a family of performers who engage in a variety of acts all over the world. A special honor was the family's induction into the Circle of Fame, an organization that recognizes circus greats.

"I began practicing as a performer when I was seven," said Eugene Nocks Jr. "I started doing what we call the sway pole, which looks like a flagpole. You climb to the top with your feet in your hands. Once you master the technique, you are, in effect, walking up the pole. It's about eighty feet in a matter of about forty-five seconds. At the age of fourteen, I had perfected the routine and began performing."

His brother John started working on his act, the pyramid of chairs, at the age of eight. As an equilibrist, or balancer, he can do handstands on as many as six chairs at one time. In other words, he makes a pyramid of all of these chairs and then balances on top of them. This is so unusual for such a young person to accomplish that he became famous when he was very young and was asked to perform on a number of television shows.

Another brother, Michael Angelo, has focused on trapezes. He started when he was an early teenager, doing front and back levers and handstands. He perfected two tricks that only a few people in the world are capable of doing: one called a one-arm back flange and another consisting of a free handstand on the trapeze.

Bello Nocks, who started working on his act at the age of six, has become a well-known clown. His knack for entertainment has led to success around the world.

The family has traveled to Australia, New Zealand, the Far East, and other spots around the world. Some members of the family speak several languages, and they have been asked to perform in a number of unusual circumstances. For instance, the Wisconsin Film Commission asked them to help in filming a Powerball commercial. The idea was to put together an amazing feat with one human catcher who would receive up to six humans at one time. With seven balls in the lottery, the one Powerball person was dressed in red and the rest were in white leotards with numbers on the front and back. It took three days to film this incredible stunt.

The group has also been hired for performances at various car races. Appearances have taken place at Daytona and the Charlotte Motor Speedway, among others.

Performances at professional baseball games have also been popular. Family members have been suspended from helicopters and have thrown the first pitch from a ninety-foot sway pole.

"Our family has been presenting this type of entertainment since, believe it or not, 1840," Bello said. "Back then, it might have been a promotional event, such as the opening of a new department store, or something of that nature. They would set up a wire from one side of the street to the other, for instance, and one of the Nocks would walk across and be the first customer."

When not performing, family members are perfecting their routines or developing new acts. Thousands of hours are spent in bringing these acts to the point where they are safe and well coordinated. A show performed at Sea World in Texas, for example, revolved around wheels. Everything in the show, which was performed six times per day, was on wheels—unicycles, bicycles, motorcycles, go-carts—all kinds of wheels. The group is always thinking about new ideas that can provide the concept for a new show. When not working on planning, they may be doing bookkeeping, sound work, or maintenance of the equipment.

To be successful in this field, Eugene Nocks said it's important for people in the entertainment business to have the right attitude and an aggressive outlook on life since they must be comfortable with large groups and be able to deal with the media. Since performers travel in large groups, they have to know how to get along with others in close quarters.

In addition, circus performers must stay in shape year-round, exercising, doing daily push-ups, chin-ups, sit-ups, and other exercises. They also need to maintain good overall health and control their diets.

"This is a most interesting business," Eugene Nocks said. "Performing is very magical, and being able to do it with other members of your family makes it even more special."

For Additional Information
American Youth Circus Organization
P.O. Box 96
Temple, NH 03084
www.americanyouthcircus.org

Circus Historical Society
600 Kings Peak Drive
Alpharetta, GA 30022
www.circushistory.org

Clowns of America International
P.O. Box Clown
Richeyville, PA 15358
www.coai.org

International Jugglers' Association
P.O. Box 112550
Carrollton, TX 75011
www.juggle.org

Bodyguards
What do the president, Britney Spears, and U2 have in common? They are all protected by bodyguards who have been assigned the responsibility of protecting their clients from any harm. This includes possible harassment, kidnapping, invasion of privacy (such as keeping adoring fans at a comfortable distance), or other types of physical or emotional distress.

The bodyguards' responsibilities may also include the protection of their clients' families or property.

Zeroing in on What a Bodyguard Does

The responsibilities of bodyguards vary, depending on the situation. In some cases, they carry weapons. In almost all cases, their effectiveness depends on both physical fitness and mental alertness.

Typically, bodyguards are part personal aide and part police officer. For example, as personal aides, they help plan and implement schedules, and as police officers, they protect the client at public or private events.

Bodyguards must always be mindful of their responsibilities. Even a moment of "letting their guard down" can bring drastic results. Being a bodyguard means remaining calm under difficult situations with an eye toward sensing possible danger. Because of the nature of this work, the stress element is very high.

Since bodyguards must stay right alongside their clients, work hours may be erratic and demanding—nights, weekends, whatever is requested. The clients always set the working hours. Sometimes, bodyguards are expected to stay for extended periods at the residences of their employers.

Often, bodyguards drive their clients from place to place and accompany them on trips. When traveling to other countries, it is important that bodyguards be familiar with the language and culture of the host country. Communication is important regardless of the location.

Bodyguards often work along with local police or other security personnel. For example, bodyguards might help develop a plan to safeguard a popular politician who is about to give a speech, while security guards would be responsible for developing a plan to safeguard the building in which the speech will take place. One individual will be assigned the task of coordinating all of the security personnel.

Qualifications and Training Required for Bodyguards

As a bodyguard, you'll often be expected to carry weapons and know how to use physical means to restrain people. The ability to think on your feet, a keen sense of attention to detail, self-control, and personal commitment are vital to your success in this profession.

It is also important for a bodyguard to have a "presence" that might discourage altercations before they get started. Sometimes emergency situations can then be avoided. The ability to plan strategies, knowledge of new surveillance techniques, and the ability to use other tactics to anticipate possible problem situations are routinely required.

Many bodyguards are former police officers. As such they have already learned how to use weapons, respond to emergencies, and control crowds. In some cases, bodyguards served in the military and gathered the necessary skills to do this kind of work. Those who have previously served as police personnel have passed stringent physical exams and exceeded the police minimum of eighteen or twenty-one years of age.

Although a college degree is usually not required, well-educated people are more likely to be successful bodyguards. This is because a well-educated person is most apt to be able to respond to rapidly developing situations in a wise manner. Also, education in psychology, law, criminal justice, or related areas allows bodyguards to perform at higher efficiency.

Of course, bodyguards must be physically fit and have sharp reflexes. This does not mean they have to be big and burly. "Lean and mean" will do fine. A number of bodyguards are trained in one or more of the martial arts as well as in first aid.

Since bodyguards are often in sensitive positions, they are often asked to pass lie detector tests before being hired. In some cases, background checks on personal and professional histories may be required.

Job Settings for Bodyguards

Anyone can obtain the services of a bodyguard, but those who call upon them predictably include movie stars, well-known musicians, political figures, and high-profile business executives. Rich and powerful people have always employed bodyguards and will undoubtedly continue to do so.

You may look for work as a bodyguard through a private security firm, a governmental agency, or direct contact with someone who seeks protection. Your chances for finding employment are greater in large cities such as New York, Miami, and Washington, D.C. Some individuals may find positions with private companies, evaluating personal security operations and offering ideas for wise changes.

Bodyguards usually get started in this business by knowing what the job entails, matching their qualifications and training to what is required, and offering their skills to a possible client. After you establish a reputation, it is possible to start your own company.

People often begin this kind of work on a part-time basis, perhaps taking on assignments while off duty as a police officer. After all, working in this capacity puts you in a perfect place to find out about bodyguard possibilities. Later, this may develop into full-time work.

Salaries for Bodyguards

Earnings for bodyguards on a part-time basis normally range from $25 to $100 per hour for routine assignments (which may extend over a period of time). Those who work full-time can expect to earn an average of $50,000 to $100,000, although a range of $25,000 to $200,000 a year is possible. Assignments that are classified or highly dangerous normally bring the higher figures. Also, if special skills such as electronic surveillance are required, wages also tend to be higher.

For those who enjoy getting close to the "rich and famous," this kind of work may be appealing. In addition, some may find it glamorous and may enjoy traveling to faraway places. Although no specific training may be required to become a bodyguard, some type of preparation is advisable. One example of training available in this area is the selection of programs provided by Executive Security International (ESI). This organization offers two thousand hours of certification programs for protection and security specialists in executive protection, protective intelligence, and investigation security specialist. Certification options include Dignitary and Executive Protection, Personal Protection, Security Specialist, and Protective Intelligence and Investigations.

Students complete much of this training through distance education, but also participate in a fifteen- or twenty-day residential training program in Aspen, Colorado.

For Additional Information

Association of International Private Investigators and
Bodyguards
www.aipib.com

Executive Security International (ESI)
Gun Barrel Square
2128 Railroad Avenue
Department Web
Rifle, CO 81650
www.esi-lifeforce.com

International Association of Professional Protection Specialists
5255 Stevens Creek Boulevard, Suite 308
Santa Clara, CA 95051
www.iapps.org

Professional Bail Agents of the United States
444 North Capitol Street
Washington, DC 20001
www.pbus.com

Secret Service Agents

Perhaps the ultimate protective roles are those performed by members of the U.S. Secret Service. When it was founded in 1865 as a branch of the U.S. Treasury Department, the original mission was to investigate counterfeiting of U.S. currency. In 1901, following the assassination of President William McKinley, the Secret Service was also assigned the responsibility of protecting the U.S. president.

By law, the Secret Service is authorized to protect the president, vice president, president-elect, vice president–elect, and their immediate family members; former presidents and their spouses; minor children of a former president until the age of sixteen; major presidential and vice presidential candidates and, within 120 days of the general election, their spouses; visiting foreign heads of government or heads of state; and others if authorized by the president.

The law authorizes Secret Service agents to carry firearms, execute warrants, make arrests, and perform other functions. Not all agents work directly in protecting the persons noted above, but for those who do, extreme diligence is required.

According to the U.S. Department of Labor, the Secret Service employs approximately twenty-one hundred special agents, twelve hundred Uniformed Division officers, and approximately seventeen hundred other technical, professional, and administrative support personnel. The Secret Service Uniformed Division is a uniformed force whose members protect the White House complex, the vice president's residence, and foreign embassies and missions in the Washington, D.C., area. Members of the

Uniformed Division also perform other missions in support of the protection of the president, such as operating magnetometers, counter snipers, canine handlers, and special operations posts. The Secret Service has agents assigned to approximately 125 offices located in cities throughout the United States and in select foreign cities.

Qualifications and Training Required for Secret Service Agents

Secret Service agents undergo intensive training. New agent trainees are first sent to the Federal Law Enforcement Training Center in Glynco, Georgia, where they are enrolled in the Criminal Investigator Training Program (CITP). This nine-week course, designed to train new federal investigators in such areas as criminal law and investigative techniques, provides a general foundation for the agency-specific training to follow.

Upon successful completion of CITP, new agent trainees attend the eleven-week Special Agent Training Course at the Secret Service Training Academy in Beltsville, Maryland. This course focuses on specific Secret Service policies and procedures associated with the dual responsibilities of investigations and protection. Trainees are provided with basic knowledge and advanced application training in combating counterfeiting, access device fraud and other financial criminal activity, protective intelligence investigations, physical protection techniques, protective advances, and emergency medicine. The core curriculum is supplemented by extensive firearms training, control tactics, water survival skills, and physical fitness.

Secret Service agents receive continuous advanced training throughout their careers. Regularly provided specialized training consists of firearms requalifications and emergency medicine refresher courses. Detail agents also participate in challenging simulated-crisis training scenarios called Attack on Principal (AOP). These exercises present agents with a variety of "real world" emergency situations involving Secret Service protectees and are designed to provide agents with immediate feedback concerning their responses to the problems.

Those agents assigned to offices in the field have the opportunity to acquire advanced training in the area of criminal investigations. Courses such as Fundamentals of Banking, Advanced Access Device Fraud, Questioned Documents, Undercover Operations, Telecommunications Fraud, and Financial Institution Fraud are generally offered as part of Secret Service training throughout the year. Agents also are encouraged to attend training sessions sponsored by other law enforcement agencies.

To qualify for the special agent position, an applicant must be a U.S. citizen and be less than thirty-seven years of age when appointed. Applicants must have a bachelor's degree from an accredited college or university or three years of work experience in criminal investigations or law enforcement fields that require knowledge and application of laws relating to criminal violations or an equivalent combination of education and related experience. Degrees in law enforcement, criminal justice, accounting, foreign languages, and computer science may be beneficial.

Secret Service special agents spend their first six to eight years on the job assigned to a field office. After the field experience, agents are usually transferred to a protective detail, where they stay for three to five years. Following the protective assignment, many agents return to the field and then transfer to a headquarters office, a training office, or an assignment based in Washington, D.C. However, promotions can affect the typical career path.

An agent's working hours depend upon the assignment. Generally, an agent can expect to travel frequently and do some shift work.

For Additional Information

For more details, contact your local Secret Service field office or the Secret Service Personnel Division, listed in the U.S. Government pages of your local telephone directory. A list of local field offices can be found at www.secretservice.gov.

··

Cowboys and Cowgirls

Does the world still need cowboys or cowgirls? In the high-tech world of the twenty-first century, there is certainly not the same level of demand for "cowpokes" as existed in the days of the Wild West, and changing times have altered the functions they perform and they way they live. But at the same time, a need still exists for workers to maintain ranches and perform related functions.

Of course, what you see in the movies is a romanticized version of the life of a cowpoke and probably bears little resemblance to the real thing. Read on to see whether you think this life is at all glamorous.

Zeroing in on What a Cowpoke Does

Ranch hands who live and work on sheep and cattle ranches spend most of their time on the range, often controlling the herd for many weeks. When away from the ranch house, they sleep in bedrolls on the ground. The equipment they need (including saddles, tack, jackets, boots, belts, hats, and spurs) can be expensive, often amounting to several thousand dollars.

Ranch hands in both the western and eastern United States may also make a living at dude ranches. Here the work is less isolating and taxing. Many responsibilities are closer to acting as professional guides or camp counselors.

For either specialty, work is largely out-of-doors and often on horseback. This is not a job for those who are averse to serious physical labor. Herding cattle on the range can be physically and mentally strenuous. Cowboys and cowgirls may also be called upon to perform other tasks such as repairing fences, general maintenance around the ranch, and caring for the horses in whatever way is necessary.

Rodeo Cowboys and Cowgirls

Some ranch hands become professional rodeo riders who travel from place to place participating in rodeo shows. This is a form of entertainment and competition based on the riding and roping skills of the Western cowboy.

The term *rodeo* is a Spanish word that denotes a gathering place of cattle or, literally, a roundup. The first formal rodeo was held in Prescott, Arizona, in 1888. Today, the modern rodeo is a colorful event that flourishes in all fifty states, most of Canada, and parts of Europe and Australia.

As the ProRodeo Hall of Fame has noted: "To some, rodeo is a sport. To others, it's a business. But to most competitors, rodeo is simply a way of life." The rodeo lifestyle and its development over the past one hundred years are vividly displayed in the ProRodeo Hall of Fame and Museum of the American Cowboy in Colorado Springs, Colorado.

Rodeo competition falls into two basic categories: rough-stock events or timed events. Rough-stock events include the scored riding events—saddle bronc riding, bull riding, and bareback riding. Cowboys must ride for a minimum of eight seconds to receive a qualified score. The timed events, which include steer wrestling, calf roping, team roping, steer roping, and barrel racing, require most contestants to ride quarter horses, and the score is based on how long it takes to complete the event.

Injury is a very real threat, and professionals often must compete in pain. In addition to this challenge, staying on the move is a necessity. In order to make a living, professionals must travel constantly across the country, particularly in the Western states.

Qualifications and Training Required for Cowboys and Cowgirls

There are no formal requirements for this career, but those considering this kind of work need to be good with horses, familiar with life on the range, comfortable with livestock, physically strong, and able to rope and assist with calving. Work may be obtained through state employment agencies or by contacting individual ranches directly.

Those interested in working at dude ranches will be helped by having experience with animals and/or experience as camp counselors or resort workers, or any jobs dealing with the public. Course work in animal husbandry, biology, and surveying is helpful.

Most ranch workers gain their credentials through on-the-job experience. Many of the best rodeo riders attended one of the top dozen or so rodeo schools in the western part of the country, where many colleges field rodeo teams. Because of the extensive physical demands of ranching and rodeo riding, those who reach their forties often seek other kinds of work.

Salaries for Cowboys and Cowgirls

This is a job that you must love because the financial rewards are not great for cowboys and cowgirls. Incomes between $400 and $1,200 a month plus room and board may be expected.

Advancement possibilities are severely limited. It is rare that someone moves up into better-paying positions such as foremen, for example, who have more responsibilities. However, those who combine practical experience with college-level study of ranch management and animal breeding will be in a position to move into supervisory roles. Ranch hands who pursue post-secondary training may be able to acquire jobs as range technicians with state and federal governments.

For rodeo cowboys and cowgirls, there are always entry fees. This means that novices are lucky if they are able to pay their travel expenses plus the entry fees. Because of this, cowboys rarely travel alone. Most take advantage of the Professional Rodeo Cowboys Association's "buddy system," which allows up to four cowboys to enter rodeos as a group and request to compete during the same show. Thus, they can travel together and share expenses. The buddy system helps make it possible for more people to participate. In the process, strong friendships usually develop even among those who compete against one another.

Most nationally ranked cowboys compete every year in 100 to 125 rodeos throughout the United States and Canada. These professionals can earn $20,000 to $40,000 or more.

In 1976, Tom Ferguson became the first cowboy in Professional Rodeo Cowboys Association history to reach $1 million in prize money. The feat took him fourteen years. Increased prize money in recent years has allowed others to rack up higher figures more rapidly.

For Additional Information

American National Cattle Women, Inc.
P.O. Box 3881
Englewood, CO 80155
www.ancw.org

Canadian Cattlemen's Association
#215, 6715 Eighth Street NE
Calgary, AB T2E 7H7
Canada
or
#1403, 150 Metcalfe Street
Ottawa, ON K2P 1P1
Canada
www.cattle.ca

Cowboy Mounted Shooting Association
14227 East Rock View Road
Scottsdale, AZ 85262
www.cowboymountedshooting.com

Dude Ranchers' Association
1122 Twelfth Street
P.O. Box 2307
Cody, WY 82414
www.duderanch.org

National Cattlemen's Beef Association
9110 East Nichols Avenue, #300
Centennial, CO 80112
www.beef.org

Professional Bull Riders, Inc.
6 South Tejon Street, Suite 700
Colorado Springs, CO 80903
www.pbrnow.com

Professional Rodeo Cowboys Association (PRCA)
101 ProRodeo Drive
Colorado Springs, CO 80919
www.prorodeo.org

Women's Professional Rodeo Association
1235 Lake Plaza Drive, Suite 127
Colorado Springs, CO 80906
www.wpra.com

Divers and Diving Instructors

Making a career out of exploring the mysteries of the deep, or enabling others to do so, may not be for everyone. But for strong swimmers who know just how exhilarating scuba diving can be, this profession is tailor made.

A variety of tasks such as construction, search and rescue, and ship repair must be done underwater. Divers who perform this work usually specialize either as scuba divers, who work just below the surface, or as deep-sea divers, who may work for long periods of time in depths up to three hundred feet.

Divers perform duties such as helping construct piers, bridges, and other structures; carrying out search-and-rescue activities; recovering sunken equipment; patrolling the waters below ships at anchor; inspecting, cleaning, and repairing ship propellers and hulls; surveying rivers, beaches, and harbors for underwater obstacles; using explosives to clear underwater obstacles; and conducting underwater research.

Such jobs certainly are a far cry from a typical office or factory environment and can hold great appeal for adventurous types who feel comfortable in the water and have the necessary physical vigor. Working as a diver also requires good powers of concentration, a high degree of self-reliance, and the ability to stay calm under stress.

According to the U.S. Department of Defense, the armed services employ more than fifteen hundred divers. Each year, they need new divers due to changes in personnel and the demands of the field. After job training, divers work in teams headed by experienced divers. Eventually, they may become master divers and supervise diving operations.

Outside the military, divers work for oil companies, salvage companies, underwater construction firms, and police or fire rescue units. Some operate their own businesses.

Zeroing in on What a Diving Instructor Does

Diving instructors teach people from all walks of life the rules of and the skills required for scuba diving. They teach safe ways of diving and provide instruction on how to best use the gear and other equipment, such as the breathing mixtures that are carried in tanks strapped to scuba divers' backs. Classes are conducted in pools, with final open-water training being conducted in rivers, oceans, lakes, and other bodies of water.

A certifying organization provides the detailed set of standards and procedures instructors must follow. These establish the guidelines for teaching techniques to students.

Sometimes scuba diving instructors also serve as underwater guides who conduct tours for divers on local reefs. Those skilled in underwater videography may provide vacationers with a taped record of their underwater escapades. Specialties such as ice diving, underwater hunting and collecting, and wreck diving may also be taught by scuba diving instructors. Law enforcement personnel, rescue workers, and firefighters may also need the services of qualified scuba instructors.

Work schedules may vary, and work may not be steady. Many instructors have only part-time schedules. Some scuba instructors employed by stores that specialize in selling scuba equipment may work forty hours a week. Usually at least one weekend a month is spent conducting final open-water instruction sessions with their students.

Unless the employer supplies it, the instructors may be responsible for buying their own equipment, which is a costly enterprise. Equipment may include fins, snorkel, boots, mask, a wet suit with gloves and hood, a buoyancy control device, lead weight belt, pressure gauge, cylinder boot, compass, underwater watch, depth gauge, diving knife, dive computer, and equipment bag. Also used are videos, textbooks, manuals, notebooks, and other teaching aids.

Qualifications and Training Required for Divers and Diving Instructors

Many divers develop their skills in the military, where their initial job training consists of five to thirteen weeks of classroom instruction, including practice in diving and repair work. Training length varies depending on specialty, with further training taking place on the job and through advanced courses. Course content typically includes principles of scuba diving, underwater welding and cutting, and maintenance of diving equipment. Civilian divers study similar topics, typically acquiring their skills through a combination of formal classes and on-the-job training.

Those with the right qualifications may move into teaching roles. To be a certified scuba diving instructor, you must have both diving and teaching skills. Requirements vary with each specific licensing agency. In most cases, you must be at least eighteen years old and have a high school diploma or GED. High school students should take cardiopulmonary resuscitation (CPR), first aid, public speaking, physics, and English.

The Professional Association of Diving Instructors (PADI) is a leading organization that trains and certifies scuba instructors. Certified divers follow four steps to become PADI open-water scuba instructors. They complete a PADI rescue diver course, a PADI divemaster course, an instructor development course, and the instructor examination.

The PADI rescue diver course is designed to teach divers how to recognize diving problems, prevent accidents, and handle diving emergencies. The divemaster course teaches divers how to supervise trained divers and how to organize and conduct diving activities. At the instructor development course, divers learn how to teach the PADI educational system in the classroom, in confined water (swimming pool), and in open water.

The final step in becoming a PADI open-water scuba instructor is the two-day instructor examination. Candidates must be able to show mastery of diving, teaching ability, group control, water skills, diver rescue, and professional attitude.

Relevant courses are also offered by the National Association of Underwater Instructors (NAUI), a nonprofit association of diving educators and businesspeople. Instruction includes swimming skills, diving skills, and scuba diving skills.

The YMCA National Scuba Program includes a progression of diver training, education, certification, and experience designed to guide an entry-level recreational diver toward a profession as a YMCA scuba instructor. After completing a series of logged dives, training in teaching techniques, demonstrating classroom instruction, and receiving a candidate evaluation, successful students are certified as YMCA scuba instructors who are qualified to teach, supervise, and evaluate student diver activity.

Job Settings for Divers and Diving Instructors

The highest concentrations of divers and diving instructors are on the West Coast and in the South, where weather conditions sustain warm temperatures, and at military bases for those in the armed services. Additional locations are Hawaii, the islands in the South Pacific, and the Caribbean. Instructors are also employed throughout the United States in retail stores that sell scuba equipment. Other possibilities for instructors include cruise ships, youth centers, theme parks, universities, military bases, and municipal aquariums.

The National Association of Underwater Instructors and the Professional Association of Diving Instructors both have placement services to help instructors find work.

Salaries for Diving Instructors

Earnings for divers vary widely. Beginning divers may earn less than $20,000 annually, while experienced divers may earn $40,000 to $80,000 a year. Earnings for instructors vary depending on the number of students, the hours of instruction, and the particular arrangement made with the diving resort, travel agency, or store where you work. Those who are employed as salespeople in stores that supply diving equipment and double as instructors often start in the $20,000 to $35,000 range. However, wages may be considerably enhanced through teaching fees and commissions on sales.

Meet a Diving Instructor

Mic McCormick, an open-water, PADI-certified instructor in Skokie, Illinois, started competitive swimming when he was five.

"I swam all through school, and in college my swim coach was also the scuba instructor, so of course I had to get into scuba," he said. "That was particularly nice because our swim team took a trip over Christmas break each year, and usually it was to Hawaii."

McCormick left college with a degree in biology and a minor both in chemistry and economics and went to work as a chemist doing environmental chemistry work. For the next few years after college, he continued to take trips and scuba dive.

After a couple of years in the industry, he started working as an engineer for a company that made environmental testing equipment. But he wasn't really happy, so he started getting into diving a little more, just to give himself a pleasurable outlet. He got to know the people at the dive center and began to work part-time for them. He liked it so much that he quit his job and became a diving instructor.

To obtain the necessary credentials, McCormick worked his way through a number of classes and levels. He became basic certified, advanced certified, and rescue certified, and then reached the level of divemaster. Following that, he was required to attend a week-long course focusing on how to teach (instructor development course). At the end of the week, he was evaluated by instructor examiners from PADI who rated his teaching presentations and his skills in the water.

"Early on, I realized one of the most important tenets of this career, that diving instructors need to be outgoing, likable, and able to work well with others," he said. "Further, the attitude needs to be, 'Hey, we can do this—if we all work together.'"

McCormick's job requires skills beyond his diving ability. "On a typical day, I arrive at about ten for a morning meeting," he said. "I help with preparations to open the store at eleven and go over my teaching schedule for that day. Since there is a considerable amount of procedure that must be followed, I often have paperwork to complete. And whenever necessary, I help customers who come into the store."

McCormick's teaching duties have included both regularly scheduled classes for groups of eight and private classes for smaller groups.

"To me, the best part of the job is having a part in seeing to it that people who are not really sure of themselves in the water become comfortable and confident enough to really enjoy all that this sport has to offer," he said.

For Additional Information

Association of Diving Contractors International
5206 FM 1960 West, Suite 202
Houston, TX 77069
www.adc-usa.org

Divemar, Inc.
6866 McKeown Drive
Greely, ON K4P 1A2
Canada
www.divemar.com

Dive Rescue International
201 North Link Lane
Fort Collins, CO 80524
www.diverescueintl.com

International Association of Dive Rescue Specialists (IADRS)
201 North Link Lane
Fort Collins, CO 80524
www.iadrs.org

International Association of Nitrox and Technical Divers
9628 Northeast Second Avenue, Suite D
Miami Shores, FL 33138
www.iantd.com

International Association of Public Safety Divers (IAPSD)
6500 Prado Boulevard
Coral Gables, FL 33143
www.publicsafetydiver.com

National Association for Search and Rescue
4500 Southgate Place, Suite 100
Chantilly, VA 20151
www.nasar.org

National Association of Underwater Instructors (NAUI)
P.O. Box 89789
Tampa, FL 33689
www.naui.com

Professional Association of Diving Instructors (PADI)
30151 Tomas Street
Rancho Santa Margarita, CA 92688
www.padi.com

Professional Diving Instructors Corporation (PDIC)
P.O. Box 3633
Scranton, PA 18505
www.pdic-intl.com

Professional Scuba Association
International Headquarters
9487 Northwest 115th Avenue
Ocala, FL 34482
www.mrscuba.com

Test Pilots

Were you enthralled with model airplanes as a child? Did you think it would be awesome to "take planes up" to make sure they were airworthy? Can you meet danger head on? Perhaps you are a good candidate to become a test pilot. Individuals who become test pilots put personal fears aside in their attempt to discover a plane's flaws before the flaws provide the impetus for a tragedy.

Zeroing in on What a Test Pilot Does

Test pilots are the pioneers who test the various aspects of an aircraft—rate of climb, staff speed, and spin characteristics, to name a few—in their quest to ascertain if the aircraft is safe. They are responsible for flying prototypes, experimental designs, and modified designs.

Like other pilots, test pilots take great care to make sure that the engines, controls, instruments, and other systems of the aircraft they fly are functioning properly. In addition, they help assess and document an aircraft's performance so that modifications in its design can be made, if necessary. In the process, they engage in takeoffs, landings, and other maneuvers, sometimes imposing extra stress on an aircraft intentionally. While in flight, they scan instruments to check matters ranging from fuel supply to the condition of engines and hydraulic systems. In completing these and other tasks, their overall goal is to determine whether an aircraft is safe and whether it is operating effectively.

Qualifications and Training Required for Test Pilots

Though not a necessity, aspiring test pilots are often individuals who have loved planes and flying since they were children. Formal schooling should include at least a bachelor's degree, most likely in mechanical, electrical, or aeronautical engineering.

The military runs an exclusive two-part, six months per part, math-intensive test pilot school, teaching abnormal flight characteristics and control as well as the precision procedures necessary to evaluate an aircraft. Most flight testing of new designs consists of taking a plane through a designated, predesigned flight program in an extremely precise maneuver.

After test pilot school, you need to fly as many hours as possible in as many different planes as possible.

Some training programs are available for those desiring to break into this field. An example is the National Test Pilot School (NTPS), a nonprofit educational institution established in 1981 to meet the specialized flight test training needs of the domestic and foreign aerospace industries and governments. NTPS bills itself as the largest civilian test pilot school in the world.

Job Settings for Test Pilots

Some test pilots work in the U.S. Air Force, Navy, or Marine Corps. After eight to ten years, many pilots leave the military and get jobs working for one of the large aircraft companies, such as Boeing, Northrop Grumman, and others.

Meet a Test Pilot

The story of test pilot Jackie Jackson is revealing. After earning a bachelor's degree in industrial management and a master's in human resources management, Jackson was far from any career that might deal with flying experimental aircraft. He worked in sales, but he did not really enjoy it. Then he ran into a friend, a former marine, who suggested that he join the U.S. Marine Corps and fly airplanes. The idea had never occurred to him before, and he had no experience in aviation. But the idea seemed interesting, and he proceeded to sign up for and pass the necessary tests.

He entered the Marine Corps Officer's Candidate School and was commissioned a second lieutenant. After earning his wings, he served in Vietnam.

"My goal was to get one thousand hours of flight time," he said, "which I managed to achieve."

While in Vietnam, he met a pilot who had been to the Naval Test Pilot School. He liked this friend's suggestion to apply to the school and applied before leaving Vietnam. After returning to the United States, he received orders to report to the Naval Test Pilot School at Petuxa River, Maryland, where he began his career as a test pilot. After several years in the military, he decided that family obligations required him to stay in the United States, so he went to work for a civilian aircraft company.

A typical day on this job started at about 7 A.M. On the three or four days a week that involved flying, he spent about an hour for a brief, an hour and a half for the flight itself, and about an hour for the debrief.

The job involved flying any of three types of projects: production flights, or flights conducted on airplanes that have just come off of the assembly line; engineering test flights, or flights conducted on proven vehicles to which some change has been made, such as a new computer or black box; or experimental flights, for aircraft that are being flown for the first time. With the latter, although wind tunnel and other extensive tests have been performed, no one ever really knows what may happen.

On days where flying was not required, he attended meetings, participated in simulations, and handled other production responsibilities. Attention was also often focused on advance programs, such as considering the options for airplanes that will be built in the future.

"Danger is a very real part of the job," Jackson admitted. As an example, he recalled "a pretty scary sixty seconds" when the plane he was flying went into an unexpected spin at thirty-seven thousand feet, and it wasn't until seventeen thousand feet that he was able to recover.

"You have to be able to react very quickly to unanticipated situations," he said. "I also feel you must have good dexterity, strong hand-eye coordination, excellent physical conditioning and overall health, a college education, the ability to write well, and the technical knowledge necessary to understand how planes and everything related to flying works."

The future looks promising for those who wish to enter this career, according to Jackson, not necessarily because of new aircraft but because of software changes in the computers of existing airplanes.

"Being a test pilot is ninety percent desire and ten percent ability," he said. "Remember, if you have the desire, you'll be able to achieve your career goals, just as I did."

For Additional Information

American Helicopter Society International
217 North Washington Street
Alexandria, VA 22314
www.vtol.org

American Institute of Aeronautics and Astronautics (AIAA)
1801 Alexander Bell Drive, Suite 500
Reston, VA 20191
www.aiaa.org

Experimental Aircraft Association
EAA Aviation Center
P.O. Box 3086
Oshkosh, WI 54903
www.eaa.org

National Test Pilot School
P.O. Box 658
Mojave, CA 93502
www.ntps.com

Society of Experimental Test Pilots
P.O. Box 986
Lancaster, CA 93584
www.setp.org

U.S. Naval Test Pilot School
22783 Cedar Point Road, Unit 21
Patuxent River, MD 20670
www.usntps.navy.mil

Most schools deal with broad-based pilot training rather than focusing on the specific needs of test pilots. For a list of certified pilot schools, write to:

Superintendent of Documents
U.S. Government Printing Office
Mail Stop SDE
732 North Capitol Street NW
Washington, DC 20401
www.gpoaccess.gov

Astronauts

There may be no more glamorous role than that of astronaut. These travelers venture where the rest of the human race can never expect to go: into the space that surrounds our world. At present this means traveling in orbit around the planet, but in the near future astronauts may return to the moon or go to Mars or other locations within the solar system.

Astronauts do more than just travel into space. They also serve as the vanguard of the scientific community in learning more about our universe. While a primary goal is learning more about the solar system and especially the portion of space in close proximity to the earth, the work of astronauts advances scientific knowledge in a wide range of disciplines. Their scientific roles may not carry the same glamour as their public personas, but this type of work provides important contributions in many areas, ranging from space medicine to weather analysis.

The space age began in the United States with the establishment of the National Aeronautics and Space Administration (NASA) in 1957. Created as a response to the launch of *Sputnik I* by the USSR, the agency's first goal was realized in 1969 when Neil Armstrong landed on the moon. Space flights became almost routine until the near tragedy of *Apollo 13*, and later the deaths of the astronauts aboard the two lost space shuttles reminded all of us how dangerous space travel can be.

Zeroing in on What an Astronaut Does

Though the word *astronaut* means "sailor among the stars," astronauts spend most of their time on the ground, learning how to operate in space and gaining knowledge of new horizons.

Once astronauts are chosen and assigned to missions, they take their places as part of space shuttle crews, which consist of at least five people: the commander, the pilot, and three mission specialists, all of whom are NASA astronauts. Some flights also call for payload specialists. Sometimes, engineers, technicians, physicians, meteorologists, or biologists are also included. Crew members are trained and cross-trained so that each one can handle at least one other associate's duties if necessary.

Pilots and commanders are pilot-astronauts who know how to fly both aircraft and spacecraft. Commanders are in charge of the overall mission. They maneuver the orbiter, supervise the crew and the operations of the vehicle, and are responsible for the success and safety of the flight. Pilots help the commanders to control and operate the orbiter and may help manipulate satellites by using a remote-control system. Like other crew members, they sometimes do work outside the craft or look after the payload.

While aboard the spacecraft, astronauts conduct experiments and other types of research under conditions of near-zero gravity. Laboratories may focus on or be related to earth sciences, astronomy, or manufacturing.

Astronauts may also be in charge of deploying, servicing, or retrieving satellites or working with meters, sensors, special cameras, or other technical equipment. While in space, astronauts are able to increase our knowledge by observing the solar system and the earth, gaining, for example, new perspectives on geological formations or pollution currents.

Qualifications and Training Required for Astronauts

In high school, it is important for would-be candidates to earn high marks and score well on standardized tests (SAT and/or ACT). The minimum degree requirement is a bachelor's degree from an accredited institution. There are many degree options in the science departments at colleges and universities. Of interest is the fact that funds are contributed by NASA to fifty-two colleges and universities through its Space Grant Consortia. If you attend any of these schools, you are ensured that the curriculum offered for space programs will conform to the guidelines NASA has established. For a list of these schools, check out the NASA website at www.nasa.gov.

No single academic field qualifies individuals to become astronauts. Generally, NASA seeks applicants who have strong technical backgrounds and excellent recommendations from undergraduate and graduate school professors who can attest to the candidates' problem-solving abilities, communicability with others, and ability to work well as part of a team.

Similarly, there are no specific age restrictions for the program. Astronaut candidates selected in the past have ranged between the ages of twenty-six and forty-six, with the average age being thirty-five. Applicants must be U.S. citizens to apply for the program through NASA, although two types of astronauts may serve who are not U.S. citizens: international astronauts and payload specialist astronauts. The countries with which the United States has an international agreement (Canada, Japan, Russia, Brazil, and Europe) select these astronauts. Each of these countries has its own space agency.

Payload specialists are persons other than NASA astronauts (pilots or mission specialists) whose presence is required on board the space shuttle to perform specialized functions related to the payload or other essential mission activities. Payload specialists are nominated by NASA, the foreign sponsor, or the designated payload sponsor (such as private companies or universities).

Flying experience is a requirement for pilot astronaut candidates, and it is also beneficial for the mission specialist astronaut candidates. The pilots selected have had military pilot training. The mission specialists with flying experience have attained it either in the military or through private lessons.

Military experience is not a requirement for the Astronaut Candidate Program. While military flight experience is advantageous for pilot astronaut candidate positions, it is not necessarily a factor for mission specialist astronaut candidate positions. In recent years, about one-third of mission specialists have been from the military, and about two-thirds have been civilians. Active duty military personnel must submit applications for the Astronaut Candidate Program through their respective service branches. After preliminary screening by the military, a small number of applications are submitted to NASA for further consideration. If selected, military personnel are detailed to NASA for a selected period of time.

In the past, astronauts have come from a variety of military and civilian backgrounds. Pilots have been chosen exclusively from a pool of high-achieving jet pilots who have accumulated more than one thousand hours of time in the air. Most pilot commanders have served or are currently serving in the armed forces. Civilian mission specialists tend to have advanced training in areas such as astronomy, biology, medicine, or mathematics.

Astronaut candidates attend classes on shuttle systems and in basic science and technology. Mathematics, geology, meteorology, guidance and navigation, oceanography, orbital dynamics, astronomy, physics, and materials processing are among the subjects. Candidates also receive training in land and sea survival training, scuba diving, and space suits.

Astronaut candidates are also required to complete military water survival training and become scuba qualified to prepare them for the extravehicular activity training. Consequently, all astronaut candidates are required to pass a swimming test during the first month of training.

Candidates are also exposed to the problems associated with high (hyperbaric) and low (hypobaric) atmospheric pressures in the altitude chambers and learn to deal with emergencies associated with these conditions. In addition, astronaut candidates are given exposure to the microgravity of space flight. A modified KC-135 jet aircraft produces periods of weightlessness for twenty seconds. During this brief period, astronauts experience the feeling of microgravity. The aircraft then returns to the original altitude and the sequence is repeated up to forty times in a day.

Pilot astronauts maintain flying proficiency by flying fifteen hours per month in NASA's fleet of two-seat T-38 jets; they build up jet aircraft hours and also practice orbiter landings in the shuttle training aircraft, a modified corporate jet aircraft. Mission specialist astronauts fly a minimum of four hours per month.

During the first year, astronaut candidates begin their formal space transportation system training program by reading manuals and by taking computer-based training lessons on the various orbiter systems ranging from propulsion to environmental control.

The next step in the training process is the single systems trainer (SST). Each astronaut is accompanied by an instructor who helps in the learning process about the operations of each orbiter subsystem using checklists similar to those found on a mission. The checklists contain information on normal system operations and corrective actions for malfunctions. The astronauts are trained in the SSTs to operate each system, to recognize malfunctions, and to perform corrective actions.

After completing the SST portion of the training program, the astronauts begin training in the complex shuttle mission simulator (SMS). The SMS provides training in all areas of shuttle vehicle operations and in all systems tasks associated with the major flight phases: prelaunch, ascent, orbit operations, entry, and landing. The orbit training includes payload operation, payload deployment and retrieval, maneuvers, and rendezvous. Two additional simulators, a fixed base and a motion base, are used to train the astronauts.

The fixed-base crew station is used for specific mission and payload training as well as launch descent and landing training. It is the only trainer with complete fore and aft consoles, including a remote manipulator system (RMS) console. A digital image generation system provides visual cues for out-the-window scenes of the entire mission, such as those of the earth, stars, payloads, and the landing runway. Missions can be simulated literally from launch to landing.

The motion-base crew station is used to train pilots and commanders in the mission phases of launch, descent, and landing. Motion cues are provided by the six-degrees-of-freedom motion system, which also allows the flight deck to be rotated ninety degrees to simulate liftoff and ascent.

Astronauts begin their training in the SMS using generic training software until they are assigned to a particular mission, approximately ten months before flight. Once they are assigned to a flight, astronauts train on a flight simulator with actual flight-specific training software. Training reaches its peak a few weeks prior to the flight when flight crew and ground controllers go through the entire mission in a joint training exercise.

During this last eleven weeks, the astronauts also train with the flight controllers in the Mission Control Center (MCC). The SMS and MCC are linked by computer in the same way the orbiter and MCC are linked during an actual mission. The astronauts and flight controllers learn to work as a team, solving problems and working nominal and contingency mission timelines. Total time in the SMS for the astronauts, after flight assignment, is about three hundred hours.

In parallel with the SMS training there are several other part-task trainers that are used to prepare astronauts for shuttle missions. These trainers are in varying degrees of fidelity and each serve a particular purpose.

The Sonny Carter Training Facility, or Neutral Buoyancy Laboratory (NBL), provides controlled neutral buoyancy operations in the facility water tank to simulate the zero-gravity, or weightless condition, that the spacecraft and crew experience during space flight. It is an essential tool for the design, testing, and development of the space station and future NASA programs. For the astronaut, the facility provides important preflight training in becoming familiar with planned crew activities and with the dynamics of body motion under weightless conditions.

Several full-scale mockups and trainers are also used to train astronauts. The full fuselage trainer is a full-sized plywood orbiter mockup with a nonfunctional mid deck and flight deck and a full-scale payload bay. It is used for onboard systems orientation and habitability training. Astronauts practice meal preparation, equipment stowage, trash management, use of cameras, and experiment familiarization. This trainer is also used for emergency egress training after shuttle landings.

The crew compartment trainer is a mockup of the forward section of the orbiter crew station, without a payload bay, that can be tilted vertically. It is used to train for on-orbit habitability procedures and also emergency pad egress and bailout operations. The crew stations of both trainers are similar. The manipulator development facility is a full-scale mockup of the payload bay with full-scale hydraulically operated RMS, the mechanical arm on the orbiter that is used to move payloads in and out of the payload bay. Mission specialists use this trainer to practice deploying payloads into the orbiter.

Pilots training for a specific mission receive more intensive instruction in orbiter approach and landing in shuttle training aircraft (STA), which are four Gulfstream II business jets modified to perform like the orbiter during landing. Because the orbiter approaches landings at such a steep angle (seventeen to twenty degrees) and high speed (over three hundred miles per hour), the STA approaches with its engines in reverse thrust and main landing gear down to increase drag and duplicate the unique glide characteristics of the Orbiter. Assigned pilots receive about one hundred hours of STA training prior to a flight, which is equivalent to six hundred shuttle approaches. In between training sessions, the crew members continue to keep themselves up-to-date on the status of the spacecraft and payloads for their missions.

In addition, the astronauts study flight rules and flight data file procedures and participate in mission-related technical meetings. They also participate in test and checkout activities at the NASA Kennedy Space Center in Florida, the launch site for the space shuttle.

If the months of preparation pay off and the mission is a success, the actual mission will have far fewer contingencies than were practiced for. The accuracy of the simulations and training is remarkable. Astronauts often comment that only the noise and vibration of launch and the experience of weightlessness are missing from the practice sessions; everything else in training accurately duplicates the space experience.

The astronauts' mission continues even after the orbiter has returned. The crew spends several days in medical testing and debriefing, recounting their experiences for the benefit of future crews to assist in future training and to add to the space flight knowledge base.

Members of the media also receive a detailed post-flight briefing by the crew. Then, the studies and training that may eventually lead to another space flight are resumed.

Job Settings for Astronauts

Pilot and mission astronauts work mainly at the Johnson Space Center in Houston, Texas. Other NASA space centers include: Ames Research Center, Moffett Field, California; Dryden Flight Research Center, Edwards, California; Goddard Space Flight Center, Greenbelt, Maryland; Marshall Space Flight Center, Huntsville, Alabama; Kennedy Space Center, Cape Canaveral, Florida; Langley Research Center, Hampton, Virginia; Jet Propulsion Laboratory, Pasadena, California; and Stennis Space Center, Bay Saint Louis, Mississippi.

At these and other locations, astronauts work in offices, training rooms, and other facilities. A major portion of their time is spent in intense training. After they attain full astronaut status, they may work in mission control or other areas, sometimes assisting in monitoring the space flights of fellow astronauts.

Salaries for Astronauts

Salaries for civilian astronaut candidates are based upon the federal government's general schedule pay scale for grades GS-11 through GS-13. The grade is determined in accordance with each individual's academic achievements and experience. Currently a GS-11 starts at $51,799 per year, and a GS-13 can earn up to $95,977 per year.

Meet an Astronaut

As a high school junior, James Arthur Lovell Jr. launched a rocket with the help of a chemistry teacher and two friends. Though it rose only eighty feet in the air and was only partially successful, Lovell knew even then that he longed for a career in rocket science. True to his ambition, Lovell became a U.S. Navy test pilot and was chosen to be an astronaut in 1962.

Lovell served as module pilot for the *Apollo 8* mission (the first manned flight to orbit the moon), as a member of the *Gemini 7* crew (in space for two weeks), with pilot Edwin Aldrin on *Gemini 12*, and as commander of *Apollo 13* in 1970. The *Apollo 13* mission was very nearly a disaster when an explosion caused the shuttle to lose oxygen and power. For four days, the world waited and prayed that somehow the astronauts would make it back home safely.

The story of the *Apollo 13* mission was made into a movie (based upon Lovell's book, originally titled *Lost Moon*) and was a box-office success, with actor Tom Hanks playing the part of

Lovell. To become familiar with the details, Hanks traveled to meet and fly with Lovell before filming.

"I tried to convey to him my feelings, my actions, my views, my goals, my inner being, so he could gain some insights and a perception of the character," Lovell said.

Lovell has said that his career was so exciting that he would have worked for NASA for nothing. "It was such an amazing and interesting job," he said. "And I wasn't the only one who felt this way. So did most of the other astronauts and a lot of other people who worked for NASA. The attrition rate at the time was almost zero because no one wanted to leave."

According to Lovell, the sense of achievement and satisfaction that astronauts experience with a job well done can be incredible, with pioneering new avenues, new vistas, and seeing things for the first time.

"*Apollo 8* was an awe-inspiring flight because my mission mates and I were the first to see the far side of the moon," he said. "So it's obviously one of the great milestones of my career."

Lovell noted that in order to become a successful astronaut, a candidate must have the following qualities: curiosity, the ability to handle stress, the facility to work well in team situations, the initiative to see problems and overcome them, sufficient training in a particular discipline such as biology or engineering, and the ability to perform optimally with only five or six hours of sleep per night. He said that it's also important to be goal oriented and persistent.

"You need to be the kind of person who is motivated to stretch to accomplish goals and be qualified and ready to enhance luck to make it work for you in the best way possible," Lovell said.

Jim Lovell predicted that NASA will continue its efforts because it has proved to be a viable, creative program. "Funding will fluctuate up and down, and the numbers of people involved may vary, but it will always attract well-qualified individuals who are motivated to explore new worlds and share in the thrill of learning things we never knew before," said Lovell.

Future Needs

Competition for astronauts is intense, and only a relatively few men and women can obtain these highly prestigious and challenging jobs. At the same time, the role of astronaut will provide exciting opportunities for those who succeed. In the future, the United States, with its international partners Japan, Canada, Russia, and the European Space Agency, will operate a manned space station. From that orbiting depot, humans will continue their journeys to the moon and Mars. As these plans become reality, the need for qualified space flight professionals will increase.

For Additional Information

National Aeronautics and Space Administration
NASA Headquarters
Washington, DC 20546
www.nasa.gov

Sky Divers

Skydiving is a sport that requires jumping out of a plane from heights up to fifteen thousand feet and opening a parachute at two thousand to twenty-five hundred feet. Sound interesting? It does to many people, and numbers show us that interest in sport jumping has really increased since World War II. There are more than two hundred thousand active sky divers in the United States and Canada today. Jumping is particularly popular in Arizona, California, Florida, and Texas.

Most people who become sky divers act out of personal interest, pursuing this activity as a sport or hobby. Some, however, turn it into a career. They master the intricacies of sport jumping and then use their skills to teach others or to work in businesses providing skydiving opportunities.

Instructors don't need any special education, but they must have two hundred jumps under their belts, attend a United States

Parachute Association (USPA) two-day seminar, obtain a doctor's certificate, and successfully complete a written examination. Manuals and course materials are provided by the USPA. Instructors must also work well with people.

Salaries in this field vary significantly. Dedicated skydiving instructors who like the sport and who work at it can make anywhere from about $35,000 to $100,000 a year.

Meet a Sky Diver

Mary Goetsch's experiences as an instructor and examiner for the United States Parachute Association, the governing United States skydiving agency, provide some interesting insights into the world of parachuting.

"You might say I was born into the world of parachute jumping," Goetsch said. "My father started jumping in the military and continued sport jumping afterwards, and my mother got tired of watching him, so she started. She even made twenty-four jumps while she was pregnant with me. They'd drag me out to the airport regularly, so I pretty much grew up there."

Goetsch's mother accumulated a total of four thousand jumps and her father about seventy-two hundred jumps. Both enjoyed serving as instructors. Her father was the senior-most instructor in the United States when he left the sport in 1993.

Goetsch began jumping when she was nineteen and received her instructor rating after she had been jumping for two years. She then attained licenses at different levels: the A license after twenty-five free falls, B license at fifty, C license at one hundred, and D license at two hundred. She also mastered three different disciplines in teaching the static-line progression method. After attaining other proficiency levels, she became an instructor and an evaluator. She also attained a pro rating and served on a skydiving team that performed public landings on pontoon boats in rivers, in atria in the middle of buildings, and in the middle of parades.

"You won't get rich doing this for a living, but I would rather be poor and be jumping out of airplanes," she said. "Very often during the summer on weekends I don't get to eat until 11:00 at night. By 7:30 in the morning, I'm either teaching or jumping."

Goetsch's career has not been without mishaps. She has broken her back, septum, and both arms, among other injuries. But she was never discouraged or dissuaded.

According to Goetsch, jumping with other people, especially first-jump course students and problem students, can be very rewarding, particularly when they are able to overcome some of their difficulties.

"Their joy becomes your joy," she said. "To accomplish this, you need to be patient, understanding, perceptive, dedicated, and compassionate. You also need to possess some strength, physical dexterity, and confidence in your own capabilities."

For Additional Information

Canadian Sport Parachuting Association
300 Forced Road
Russell, ON K4R 1A1
Canada
www.cspa.ca

Christian Skydivers Association
P.O. Box 1451
Valrico, FL 33595
www.members.aol.com/christskyd

National Skydiving League
1100 Biscayne Boulevard
Deland, FL 32724
www.skyleague.com

Parachute Industry Association
3833 West Oakton Street
Skokie, IL 60076
www.pia.com

River Rafting Guides

If the thought of journeying down picturesque, mysterious rivers and actually getting paid for it sounds appealing to you, think about taking up a career as a river rafting guide. This occupation combines the chance to work in beautiful surroundings with an active and challenging daily routine.

Zeroing in on What a River Rafting Guide Does

For rafters, the journey is often much more important than the destination. With the ever-increasing emphasis on nature and the outdoors, this sport has become more and more popular. There are twenty-two major and numerous minor rivers that can be rafted on the East Coast, and in the West, serious rafters are found on any moving waterway, including rivers along the Rocky and Cascade mountain ranges.

Those devoted to rafting tend to buy their own equipment, but those who raft only occasionally or are new to it generally run rivers through outfitting companies. To protect both their investments and the lives of their customers, these companies often employ river guides who are familiar with both raft handling and the intricacies of white water.

Generally, guides are trained in the early spring before the beginning of the busy season. They are taught how to navigate the branches of the rivers, with an emphasis on noting eddies, rocks, and currents. Rapids are evaluated according to their difficulty, with Class I being the most placid and Classes V and VI being the most dangerous. Most tours are for Class IV and below, but even these can be risky.

Guides must also repair and maintain equipment and be prepared to deal with sudden rainstorms or individuals who fall in the water and show signs of hypothermia. Other responsibilities include unpinning rafts, throwing ropes, and handling launchings. Hours are long and work can be rigorous. Trips may last a few hours or several days.

Qualifications and Training Required for River Rafting Guides

Guides should love the outdoors, enjoy working with people, and be certified as emergency medical technicians, which involves taking a 120-hour Red Cross course in first aid and rescue. They should also be familiar with boat navigation, maintenance, and repair as well as with camping and outdoor cooking techniques. It is also worthwhile to become knowledgeable about fishing, river lore, geology, and history.

Training is available from commercial white-water schools, specialized outdoor equipment shops, and white-water clubs. Even some colleges and universities offer courses.

Entrance into the field may be gained through a recommendation of someone who is working as a guide already or by becoming involved with the sport and a particular store affiliated with the sport. Those already employed as guides may provide recommendations for full-time positions. You may also enroll in a professional guiding course that is offered by various companies. Courses can cost several hundred dollars with no guarantee of a job upon completion, but many firms only hire from among those who have taken the course.

Salaries for River Rafting Guides

During the season, a guide may earn about $40 to $100 per day. As a head guide, the pay may exceed $115 per day.

For Additional Information

American Canoe Association
7432 Alban Station Boulevard, Suite B-232
Springfield, VA 22150
www.acanet.org

American Recreation Coalition
1225 New York Avenue NW, Suite 450
Washington, DC 20005
www.funoutdoors.com

America Outdoors
P.O. Box 10847
Knoxville, TN 37939
www.ao-directory.com

Professional Paddlesports Association (PPA)
7432 Alban Station Boulevard, Suite B-244
Springfield, VA 22150
www.propaddle.com

The Trade Association of Paddlesports (TAPS)
P.O. Box 6353
Olympia, WA 98507
www.gopaddle.org

USA Canoe/Kayak
230 South Tryon Street, Suite 220
Charlotte, NC 28202
www.usack.org

CHAPTER FOUR

Careers Involving Animals

Courage is resistance to fear, mastery of fear—not absence of fear.
—Mark Twain

Help Wanted: Individual to Work with Bees or Exotic Animals

Sound interesting? How well do you relate to bees, zoo animals, or other creatures? This chapter tells you what it's like to work with these creatures on a daily basis. Such work may not involve the same kind of courage as jumping out of airplanes or blasting into space, but it can provide a real change of pace from more "ordinary" occupations.

Beekeeping

Modern beekeeping, or apiculture, is based on the ancient Greek technique of creating a so-called bee space. In the United States, a beehive based on this ancient principle was developed by Lorenzo Lorraine Langstroth in 1851. Beekeeping became a popular activity after that time, continuing into the present.

According to *Bee Culture* magazine, there are about ninety thousand beekeepers in the United States. About eighty thousand of those are hobbyists, with most of the remainder maintaining hives as a sideline to some other business enterprise, and about one thousand operating as commercial producers.

The main objective of beekeepers is harvesting honey. According to the U.S. Department of Agriculture, honey production from producers with five or more bee colonies totaled more than 170 million pounds in 2002. All told, beekeepers maintained more than 2.5 million honey-producing colonies. Their efforts not only provide honey, but also support agriculture in general though the pollination of crops performed by bee populations.

Although bee stings pose risks to humans (especially for those who are allergic to them), working with bees is not really dangerous. However, people sensitive to bee venom should not become beekeepers.

Zeroing in on What a Beekeeper Does

The typical beehive consists of a bottom board and several boxes containing movable frames and a cover. Each frame is furnished with a beeswax foundation imprinted with the hexagonal shapes of cell bottoms. The bees, guided by the imprinted cells, use the beeswax foundation to build their honeycombs.

Spring is the time to set up new hives or take care of old ones. To start new hives, beekeepers build and paint the special wooden hives. Usually, beekeepers buy a package of bees (two or three pounds of bees and one queen) from a dealer. When the bees settle in, beekeepers screen the entrance and move the colony to an orchard, clover field, or other place where the bees can find nectar. The hives should be on a slight rise of ground with a sunny exposure and protected from strong winds and rain. Bottom boards should be raised above the bare ground.

Beekeepers keep an eye on the quantity of honey the bees are producing and regularly inspect hives to make sure they are not crowded and that they are clean and free of disease and parasites. If there is any trace of a problem, beekeepers use drugs and chemicals recommended by state agricultural departments or agricultural agents.

If an entire colony is diseased, it must be destroyed by burning the frames (combs) and killing the bees.

To examine a hive, a beekeeper uses a smoker, which calms the bees by blowing smoke into the hive entrance. Then the beekeeper opens the hive and examines each honeycomb, checking the brood (eggs and larvae) in the combs. If a queen is weak and not producing enough brood, the keeper may replace her with a young queen bee.

Among the thousands of bee species, honeybees are one of several that live in colonies. The bees gather nectar and pollen from flowers and make honey from the nectar. They store it as food for the winter or feed it to the young bees.

Honeybees hunt for nectar for two miles in all directions from their hive. They may forage over twenty thousand acres, and as they go from blossom to blossom, they transfer pollen and help plants reproduce. About one-third of all the food Americans eat depends on pollination by bees.

Most beekeepers work with the Italian honeybee, a gentle and hardworking species. Another European bee, the Carniolan, is also quite gentle yet still able to withstand hard winters. Bees may survive as long as six months during the winter, when they are less active, whereas hardworking summers may only allow a life span of four to six weeks. The cycle continues because a new generation is always available to take over and continue the colony.

Under good management, honeybees make much more honey than they need for themselves. Each hive contains a queen bee to lay eggs, hundreds of drones for reproduction, and forty to fifty thousand worker bees. In a successful season, a colony of bees will produce about 100 to 125 pounds of extra honey. Beekeepers gather the surplus honey and sell it.

Beekeepers often work long hours. During the summer and spring months when the honey is flowing and is ready to be harvested, beekeepers may need to work weekends and holidays to process and prepare the honey and other products for sale. The winter months generally allow for more leisure time.

Stings are a hazard, but beekeepers wear protective clothing and know when and how to examine hives without exciting the bees. For instance, the bees are defensive in rainy weather and potentially more aggressive at night, early in the morning, or late in the afternoon.

Beekeepers must buy tools and equipment. Besides hives and bees, they need tools to remove the combs from a hive, a storage tank, an extractor, and filtering and bottling equipment.

A number of regional and national beekeeping groups serve both hobbyists and commercial beekeepers as well as related professionals. For instance, members of the American Beekeeping Federation include honey producers, packers, shippers, and suppliers.

Qualifications and Training Required for Beekeepers

High school courses such as agriculture, biology, general business, and wood shop are useful to future beekeepers. Interested individuals may obtain the skills and knowledge necessary for raising bees on a commercial scale in any of the following ways: by completing apiculture courses offered by certain junior and senior colleges, technical schools, and extension services; by gaining full- or part-time employment with established beekeepers and becoming skilled through on-the-job training; or through individual study.

Beekeepers with bachelor's degrees in entomology and beekeeping experience may work as state inspectors. Those with doctorates may do research for the U.S. Department of Agriculture or state universities.

Information on the availability of training opportunities in your area can be obtained from your county agricultural agent, school guidance counselor, local offices of the U.S. Department of Agriculture, and state agricultural colleges. Libraries have books and other sources of information on this topic also.

Personal traits needed for this career include mechanical aptitude, good judgment and business sense, patience and alertness, an orderly mind, steady nerves, a liking for out-of-doors activities, and the ability to organize and plan work activities.

Good health, at least average physical strength, and full use of the hands, arms, legs, and back are necessary in this career. You also should have a strong sense of smell, hearing, sight, and taste in order to detect problems within the colonies.

Job Settings for Beekeepers

Beekeepers are often self-employed professionals who work out-doors year round. Time is also spent indoors cleaning and maintaining equipment and keeping business records. If they have a large number of hives in several places, beekeepers travel from place to place.

Beekeepers who supply bees for crop pollination live near the farmers who rent their hives. Honeybees pollinate crops nation-wide. They serve alfalfa fields, almond and apple orchards, and crops such as blueberries, strawberries, cherries, cantaloupes, cucumbers, watermelons, peas, beans, clover, and cut-flower seed fields.

Beekeepers may need a permit to keep hives in certain places. Many towns restrict the number of hives in residential sections. And some regions keep track of the number of hives for honeybee disease control and to make sure there are not too many bees foraging on the acreage. County extension offices and state agricultural colleges can usually provide that information for interested parties. Local beekeepers and bee supply firms may be identified by perusing the yellow pages of the phone book or, when applicable, checking out websites.

Salaries for Beekeepers

The earnings of beekeepers vary with the number of hives, the crops being pollinated, weather conditions, the yield of honey (which varies from season to season), the cost of running the business, and the knowledge and skill of the beekeeper. Beekeeping as a full-time business requires a large number of hives. One hive, in a good season, can produce as much as 200 pounds of honey. Yields for commercial beekeepers usually range from 100 to 125 pounds a hive. Income for beekeepers may range from $10,000 to $20,000 a year. Managers of large bee companies may earn $20,000 to $40,000 a year or more.

Beekeepers who rent their hives to farmers and others for pollination purposes can earn a substantial amount unless the cost of moving the hives is too great. The rental fee may be from $20 to $50 or more per hive.

For Additional Information

American Beekeeping Federation
P.O. Box 1337
Jesup, GA 31598
www.abfnet.org

Canadian Honey Council
Suite 236, 234-5149 Country Hills Boulevard NW
Calgary, AB T3A 5K8
Canada
www.honeycouncil.ca

National Honey Board
390 Lashley Street
Longmont, CO 80501
www.nhb.org

Animal Trainers and Zookeepers

If bees don't appeal to you, how about lions? Or tigers? Or bears?

Some courageous types find themselves training these or other animals for circuses, television shows, or movies. Or they fill other roles that involve working with animals, some of which require more courage than others.

Zeroing in on What Animal Trainers and Zookeepers Do

Certainly, training or simply taking care of animals can be hard work. Animal care and service workers (who include animal care-takers and animal trainers) train, feed, water, groom, bathe, and exercise animals, and clean, disinfect, and repair their cages. They also play with the animals, provide companionship, and observe behavioral changes that could indicate illness or injury. Boarding kennels, animal shelters, veterinary hospitals and clinics, stables, laboratories, aquariums, and zoological parks all house animals and employ animal care and service workers.

Some of these jobs, such as those of kennel attendants, groomers, or veterinary technicians, may not fit into the courageous category. Others, such as zookeepers and animal trainers, can involve working with animals that are potentially much more dangerous than the average cat or dog.

Animal care and service workers in zoos, called keepers, prepare the diets and clean the enclosures of animals and sometimes assist in raising them when they are very young. They watch for any signs of illness or injury, monitor eating patterns or any changes in behavior, and record their observations. Keepers also may answer questions and ensure that the visiting public behaves responsibly toward the exhibited animals. Depending on the zoo, keepers may be assigned to work with a broad group of animals, such as mammals, birds, or reptiles, or they may work with a limited collection of animals, such as primates, large cats, or small mammals.

Animal trainers focus on training animals for riding, security, performance, obedience, or assisting persons with disabilities. They do this by accustoming the animal to human voice and contact and conditioning the animal to respond to commands. Trainers use several techniques to help them train animals. One technique, known as a bridge, is a stimulus that a trainer uses to communicate the precise moment an animal does something correctly. When the animal responds correctly, the trainer gives positive reinforcement in a variety of ways: food, toys, play, rub-downs, or speaking the word *good*. Animal training takes place in small steps and often takes months and even years of repetition. During the conditioning process, trainers provide animals with mental stimulation, physical exercise, and husbandry care. In addition to their hands-on work with the animals, trainers often oversee other aspects of the animal's care, such as diet preparation. Trainers often work in competitions or shows, such as the circus or marine parks. Trainers who work in shows also may participate in educational programs for visitors and guests.

Job Settings for Animal Trainers and Keepers

Generally, people who love animals get satisfaction from working with and helping them. However, some of the work may be unpleasant, as well as physically and emotionally demanding, and sometimes dangerous. Most animal care and service workers have to clean animal cages and lift, hold, or restrain animals, risking exposure to bites or scratches. Their work often involves kneeling, crawling, repeated bending, and lifting heavy supplies, such as bales of hay or bags of feed. Animal caretakers must take precautions when treating animals with germicides or insecticides. The work setting can be noisy. Caretakers of show and sports animals sometimes travel to competitions.

Animal care and service workers may work outdoors in all kinds of weather. Hours are irregular. Animals have to be fed every day, so caretakers often work weekend and holiday shifts. In some animal hospitals, research facilities, and animal shelters, an attendant is on duty twenty-four hours a day, which means night shifts. The majority of full-time animal care and service workers work about forty hours a week.

Animal trainers and keepers may work for zoos, theme parks, circuses, and other amusement and recreation services. Some are self-employed. Employment of animal trainers tends to be concentrated in animal services that specialize in training horses and pets, as well as in commercial sports, training racehorses and dogs.

Qualifications and Training Required for Animal Trainers and Keepers

According to the U.S. Department of Labor, most animal care and service workers are trained on the job. Employers generally prefer to hire people who have some experience with animals.

Animal trainers often need to possess a high school diploma or GED equivalent. However, some animal training jobs may require a bachelor's degree and additional skills. For example, a marine mammal trainer usually needs a bachelor's degree in biology, marine biology, animal science, psychology, zoology, or a related field, plus strong swimming skills and scuba certification. All animal trainers need patience, sensitivity, and experience with problem solving and obedience. Certification is not mandatory, but several organizations offer training programs and certification for prospective animal trainers.

Some zoological parks may require their caretakers to have a bachelor's degree in biology, animal science, or a related field. Most require experience with animals, preferably as a volunteer or paid keeper in a zoo. Zookeepers may advance to senior keeper, assistant head keeper, head keeper, and assistant curator, but few openings occur, especially for the higher-level positions.

Animal caretaker jobs that require little or no training often have flexible work schedules. As a result, these jobs may be attractive to students and others looking for temporary or part-time work.

An unusual training opportunity in this area is offered by California's Moorpark College through its Exotic Animal Training and Management (EATM) program, which has been in operation since 1974. A professor at Moorpark College started the program with one animal, and as more animals were added over the years, a special compound was constructed to house them. Students have always been the primary caretakers of these animals, which at various times have included elephants, alligators, tigers, lions, hyenas, sea lions, camels, and other creatures.

The college, which calls its present five-acre animal facility "America's Teaching Zoo," requires students in the program to work at the facility in addition to attending classes. Program graduates are now working around the world in jobs such as training dolphins and other marine mammals, training animals for television and films, and working at zoos and theme parks.

For more information, contact the college at:

Moorpark College
7075 Campus Road
Moorpark, CA 93021
www.moorparkcollege.edu

Salaries for Animal Trainers and Keepers

According to the U.S. Department of Labor, median hourly earnings of nonfarm animal caretakers were $7.67 in 2000. The middle 50 percent earned between $6.48 and $9.59. The bottom 10 percent earned less than $5.78, and the top 10 percent earned more than $12.70 per hour.

Median hourly earnings of animal trainers were $10.54 in 2000. The middle 50 percent earned between $7.59 and $16.19. The lowest 10 percent earned less than $6.25, and the top 10 percent earned more than $20.85 per hour.

For Additional Information

American Society for the Prevention of Cruelty to Animals (ASPCA)
424 East Ninety-Second Street
New York, NY 10128
www.aspca.org

American Zoo and Aquarium Association
8403 Colesville Road, Suite 710
Silver Spring, MD 20910
www.aza.org

International Association of Canine Professionals (IACP)
P.O. Box 560156
Montverde, FL 34756
www.dogpro.org

International Marine Animal Trainers Association
1200 South Lake Shore Drive
Chicago, IL 60605
www.imata.org

Fishing and Hunting Guides

Fishing and hunting are hobbies enjoyed by millions of people every year. In addition to the challenge of the "catch," people often richly value these experiences because of the calm and inner peace that comes with getting away from hectic daily schedules and entering the serene, picturesque landscape provided by nature. To obtain the maximum level of enjoyment, both novices and those with more experience are often willing to pay hefty fees to qualified guides who can take them to the best fishing or hunting locations. This demand supports the career interests of men and women who love the outdoors sufficiently to make it an occupational focus.

Outdoor guides don't work with animals in the same way that animal trainers or keepers do, but they still must have a broad understanding of wild animals and their habitats. The need for their services can provide challenging career options for the right type of person.

Zeroing in on What a Fishing or Hunting Guide Does

Fishing and hunting aficionados hire guides so that they may reap the greatest rewards from the limited time and money they have to give to their chosen sport. All responsibilities then shift to the guides, who must plan the itinerary and then lead the party members through the expedition without incident.

For inexperienced hunters or anglers, the guides serve as teachers, showing clients the best ways to handle fishing equipment and guns in a safe and skillful manner.

Much planning goes into making sure that the trip will proceed smoothly and successfully. Guides must assure that each individual has the proper gear (clothing, footgear, weapons, cooking utensils, and supplies) and knows what to expect from the excursion. Additionally, guides are responsible for setting up the campsites, cooking the meals, and leading the group to fish or gaming areas. When not on trips, guides take care of paperwork and repair any equipment necessary.

Performing this kind of work has many advantages, not the least of which is leading a simple existence amid breathtaking surroundings. It is not, however, a life for those who mind "roughing it." There are few comforts of home at your disposal in the wild.

Qualifications and Training Required for Fishing or Hunting Guides

Individuals drawn to this profession enjoy the outdoors, nature, and wildlife. Often these are people who had pleasurable childhood experiences with hunting, fishing, riding horses, or operating boats. Many participated in well-known groups such as Boy Scouts, Girl Scouts, 4-H clubs, or similar organizations.

At the high school or college level, course work in biology, ecology, and photography may be helpful. Some states require that guides know how to swim, how to provide first aid and CPR, and how to practice navigation methods. And it is mandatory for guides to have knowledge of fishing and gaming laws. Sometimes state conservation departments offer practical courses, such as conservation of natural resources, hunting and fishing skills, and hunter safety.

Personal qualifications for guides include strength, good health, endurance, alertness, handiness, patience, good eyesight and hearing, and the ability to take care of fishing equipment, boats, and guns.

Licensing (with accompanying fees) varies from state to state, but in all cases candidates must be at least eighteen years old. In some states, passage of oral or written tests is required. Licenses may be renewed yearly if there have been no legal infractions.

Job Settings for Hunting or Fishing Guides

In certain states, such as Wyoming and Montana, hunting and fishing guides must work under the direct supervision of a licensed outfitter. Outside the Rocky Mountain region, guides work as self-employed entrepreneurs. As such, they set their own hours and rates. Trips may vary from a few hours to several days.

Salaries for Hunting or Fishing Guides

Wages depend on the guide's skills and ability to secure clients. A guide may average from $800 to $1,600 per month, and sometimes more.

California, Florida, and the Great Lakes states tend to have the most work for charter boat captains and guides. A daily fee of $400 or more for boat and services may be paid for groups of four to six people.

Meet a Fishing Guide

Peter Linsner became a guide after a radical change in occupations. As a communications tower builder/climber on a construction site, he was on the ground working on an antenna when a coworker dropped a twelve-inch wrench from his pouch and it fell sixty feet and hit Linsner in the head. Since he wasn't wearing a helmet, the wrench impaled his head. In a coma for nine days, he awoke to find his right side paralyzed. He couldn't walk or talk, so he had to undergo speech therapy, physical therapy, occupational therapy, and therapeutic recreational therapy to learn how to walk and talk all over again.

Before the injury, he had worked with people with disabilities at Touch of Nature, a summer camp for those with cerebral palsy, muscular dystrophy, and head injuries, and at the Center for Comprehensive Services, a facility involved with adults and adolescents with traumatic brain injuries. Since he already had a background in recreation and liked working with people with disabilities, he went back to school at a community college and earned an associate's degree in recreational therapy. One of his instructors recommended that he continue his studies, so he went on to earn a bachelor's degree.

With money from a legal settlement resulting from his head injury, he designed a boat, purchased a hull, and had a friend who was a welder build a side door onto the boat so he could bring the boat to the person rather than the other way around. The boat was wheelchair accessible, with room for another friend or caretaker. With the purchase of special equipment such as electric fishing reels, harnesses, rod holders, and adaptive handles for people with limited mobility or fine dexterity movement, he was all set to launch his own business.

"I provide all the equipment, including lunch or refreshments if requested, and whatever assistance is necessary," Linsner said. "This includes lessons on how to fish, how to use a life vest, and how to enjoy wildlife such as birds, deer, beaver, and loons. I teach about environmental concerns and record the day's experiences with a camera. If anyone catches a sizable fish, I put a notice in one of the fishing magazines that I subscribe to or advertise in."

Though his target population is people with disabilities, he also serves other customers.

"I really love what I do and consider myself to be very lucky," he said. "The joy I witness through smiles and laughs are moments you can't put a price on. This is not the kind of business that makes you rich, but I'm happy."

For Additional Information

Outdoor Guides Association
P.O. Box 12996
Tallahassee, FL 32317
www.wwwdi.com/oga

CHAPTER FIVE

Careers in Law Enforcement

All our dreams come true—if we have the courage to pursue them.
—Walt Disney

I n recent years, American voters have made it clear that they want government to place great emphasis on efforts to reduce serious crime through law enforcement. As one response to this, law enforcement officers have become more involved and visible in communities, particularly in high-crime, urban neighborhoods. This serves to increase public confidence in the police and mobilizes the public to help police fight crime.

Law Enforcers

Throughout the United States and Canada, people in all walks of life depend on police officers to protect their lives and property. Law enforcement officers, some of whom are state or federal special agents or inspectors, perform these duties in a variety of ways, depending on the size and type of their organizations. In most jurisdictions, they are expected to exercise authority when necessary, whether on or off duty. According to U.S. Bureau of Justice statistics, about 65 percent of state and local law enforcement officers are uniformed personnel.

Uniformed police officers who work in municipal police departments of various sizes, small communities, and rural areas have general law enforcement duties. This includes maintaining regular patrols and responding to calls for service. They may direct traffic at the scene of a fire, investigate a burglary, or give first aid to an accident victim. In large police departments, officers usually are assigned to a specific type of duty. Many urban police agencies have become more involved in community policing, a practice in which an officer builds relationships with the citizens of local neighborhoods and mobilizes the public to help fight crime.

A number of special police agencies also employ police officers. Examples include public colleges and universities, public school districts, and agencies serving transportation systems and facilities. More than 75 percent of the sworn personnel in special agencies are uniformed officers, and about 15 percent are investigators. According to the U.S. Department of Labor, about 10 percent of local and special law enforcement officers perform jail-related duties, and around 4 percent work in courts. Regardless of job duties or location, police officers and detectives at all levels must write reports and maintain meticulous records that are needed if they testify in court.

Zeroing in on What a Police Officer Does

Police officers working in smaller communities and rural areas are usually given varied responsibilities for handling general law enforcement duties. In the course of a day's work, they may investigate a burglary, direct traffic at the scene of a fire, or give first aid to an accident victim. In larger police departments and federal agencies, officers and special agents usually are assigned to a specific detail for a fixed length of time. Some may become experts in chemical and microscopic analysis or handwriting and fingerprint identification. They may also serve as members of the mounted or motorcycle patrol, harbor patrol, canine corps, special weapons and tactics (SWAT) groups, or task forces formed to combat specific types of crime.

Most new police recruits begin their careers in urban settings, where they often are initiated by serving on patrol duty, riding in a police vehicle. In smaller agencies, they may work alone; in larger agencies, they ride with experienced officers. Patrols generally cover a specific area, perhaps an old and congested business district or outlying residential neighborhood. Officers strive to become very familiar with conditions throughout their patrol areas and, while on patrol, remain alert for anything unusual. They note suspicious circumstances, such as open windows or lights in vacant buildings, as well as hazards to public safety. Officers on patrol enforce traffic regulations while keeping an eye out for stolen vehicles or wanted individuals. On a regular basis, officers report to police headquarters by radio or telephone.

Meet a Police Officer

For a look at the work of a patrolman in a village police department located near a large metropolitan city, consider the experience of Michael Untirdt.

"I became interested in this career at the college level when I began taking courses at Western Illinois University," said Untirdt. "I especially found classes about law interesting, so I made that my major and graduated with a bachelor's degree in law enforcement." Another consideration that drew him to this type of work was that he would be out in the streets among people rather than sitting behind a desk all day.

During his last semester of college, when he was required to complete an internship, Untirdt chose to do his with a police department. He found this to be very valuable because it provided a realistic view of what the job entailed. He was exposed to all the shifts, record keeping, radio operation, and other tasks related to being a policeman.

Untirdt said that to some, the daily schedule of a police officer in his department may seem somewhat boring. A great deal of time is spent driving around patrolling, being on the alert for individuals who are breaking the law or who look suspicious, as if they have something to hide. The rest of the time is spent responding to calls from the public and filling out reports.

In his area, where crime rates are low, police officers handle relatively few rapes, homicides, or domestic violence calls. At the same time, they must always be ready to handle such situations in the event they occur.

According to Untirdt, candidates for this career area must meet the requirements set by each agency, which may vary from one to another. A high school diploma is normally required, although college experience is becoming more and more desirable. A minimum age (eighteen or twenty-one) is also common.

Applicants who successfully pass all preliminary tests are typically sent to police academies. Chosen candidates attend for periods such as ten or twelve weeks, although some recruits may stay longer to receive additional instruction that is specific to procedures in a particular police agency.

"Besides formal training at the academy, I believe police officers need to have common sense and the ability to relate well to all kinds of people," Untirdt said. "This requires them to show compassion, understanding, and a healthy respect for the plight of others."

One way to explore an interest in this career is to look into the ride-along program that many towns offer, Untirdt noted.

"Try to take advantage of this opportunity by going along, particularly on differing shifts," he said. "Try to put yourself in this police officer's shoes. Ask some questions as you ride along. Imagine yourself doing this kind of work for the next twenty or twenty-five years. Though it may be hard to project yourself so far into the future, this is a good opportunity to find out if police work is truly your calling."

Meet a SWAT Team Member

Some police also take on the special role of SWAT team member. That was the path followed by David Jenkins, a highly experienced law enforcement veteran who also developed special skills as a member of the Northern Illinois Police Alarm System (NIPAS), a special weapons and tactics (SWAT) team.

Jenkins started out in the military and then worked as a security officer for a school district. He then became a police officer. Working as both a detective and a patrolman, he completed special training to become a member of the SWAT team. This included a spot on the entry team (a team of ten who are trained to go in first), a role as a marksman (or sniper), and a stint in tactical intelligence doing background information and training for the fifty-man team.

"When SWAT teams are called in, the situations are all potentially dangerous; otherwise, they would have been handled by the local law enforcement community," he said. "Our particular SWAT team represents a unique situation in that it is a blending of men from seventy-five towns. Manpower is combined in order to have a substantial team, which is then at the disposal of any of the seventy-five member towns."

According to Jenkins, anyone interested in SWAT team work must have experience as a police officer first. In his department, at least five years of experience on the street is needed before a police officer can apply. Applicants go through a rigorous selection process before the successful candidates are chosen and assigned to training. The screenings include a physical agility test and psychological tests. Those who pass go into a two-week basic training period with the NIPAS team, and training continues in an ongoing fashion throughout the year.

"SWAT team members are on call twenty-four hours a day, seven days a week," Jenkins said. Each member of the team carries a pager, and if a situation occurs and the team is called out, members are notified by the dispatch center, which puts out a message via their pagers. This has nothing to do with working their regular shifts as police professionals in their regular assignments. If a situation comes up during a shift, Jenkins immediately grabs his gear and heads to the SWAT destination.

"If they need to replace me, they will send someone to take my regular assignment," he explained. "If I'm home, I have to have my pager on at all times. If they call me out during the night, I just respond to the incident from my home. There is no full-time SWAT team, so we are called in when there is a serious situation that other law enforcers are not equipped to handle, such as natural disasters, drug raids, serving high-risk warrants, hostage situations, or riots."

Jenkins has had to contend with men brandishing machetes, kids building bombs and threatening to blow themselves up, and individuals with rifles who were threatening family members or other people. He and his peers have been called to locations where individuals have actually been in the process of shooting people and barricading themselves, sometimes with and sometimes without hostages.

"SWAT work is very demanding," he said. "You must do a lot of sacrificing. You must really have your personal life in order because there's a lot of responsibility to this job."

Jenkins noted that when a situation has been handled without firing a shot, that is considered a successful resolution. "All law enforcers are interested in protecting and serving, and we want everyone to go home safe and sound," he said. "If things work out that way, we have truly fulfilled our goal."

Sheriffs and Deputy Sheriffs

Sheriffs and deputy sheriffs enforce the law on the county level. Sheriffs are usually elected to their posts and perform duties similar to those of a local or county police chief. Sheriff's departments tend to be relatively small, most having fewer than twenty-five sworn officers. A deputy sheriff in a large agency will have law enforcement duties similar to those of officers in urban police departments.

Nationwide, about 40 percent of full-time sworn deputies are uniformed officers assigned to patrol and respond to calls, 12 percent are investigators, 30 percent are assigned to jail-related duties, and 11 percent perform court-related duties, according to the U.S. Department of Labor. Most of the rest work in administration.

Police and sheriff's deputies who provide security in city and county courts are sometimes called bailiffs.

State Police Officers

State police officers (sometimes called state troopers or highway patrol officers) arrest criminals on a statewide basis and patrol highways to enforce motor vehicle laws and regulations. Uniformed officers are most visible when they issue traffic citations to motorists who violate the law. At the scene of accidents, they may direct traffic, give first aid, and call for emergency equipment. They also write reports used to determine the cause of the accident.

In addition to patrolling highways, state police enforce criminal laws. They are frequently called upon to render assistance to officers of other law enforcement agencies. In rural areas that do not have a police force or a local representative from the sheriff's department, the state police are the primary law enforcement officers, investigating any crimes that occur, such as burglary or assault.

State law enforcement agencies operate in every state except Hawaii. Seventy percent of the full-time sworn personnel in the forty-nine state police agencies are uniformed officers who regularly patrol and respond to calls for service. Fifteen percent are investigators; 2 percent are assigned to court-related duties; and the remaining 13 percent work in administrative or other assignments, according to the Department of Labor.

Detectives and Federal Agents

Detectives are plainclothes investigators who gather facts and collect evidence for criminal cases. Some are assigned to interagency task forces to combat specific types of crime. They conduct interviews, examine records, observe the activities of suspects, and participate in raids or arrests. Detectives and state and federal agents and inspectors usually specialize in one of a wide variety of violations, such as homicide or fraud. They are assigned cases on a rotating basis and work on them until an arrest and conviction occurs or the case is dropped.

U.S. Drug Enforcement Administration (DEA) agents enforce laws and regulations relating to illegal drugs. Not only is the DEA the lead agency for domestic enforcement of federal drug laws, it also has sole responsibility for coordinating and pursuing U.S. drug investigations abroad. Agents may conduct complex criminal investigations, carry out surveillance of criminals, and infiltrate illegal drug organizations using undercover techniques.

U.S. marshals and deputy marshals protect the federal courts and ensure the effective operation of the judicial system. They provide protection for the federal judiciary, transport prisoners, protect witnesses, and manage assets seized from criminal enterprises. They enjoy the widest jurisdiction of any federal law enforcement agency and are involved to some degree in nearly all federal law enforcement efforts. In addition, U.S. marshals apprehend fugitives and operate the Special Operations Group (SOG), a tactical unit that responds to high-threat and emergency situations. Some deputies provide security to the Department of Defense and the U.S. Air Force during movements of missiles between military facilities.

U.S. Immigration and Naturalization Service (INS) agents and inspectors facilitate the entry of legal visitors and immigrants to the United States and detain and deport those arriving illegally. They consist of border patrol agents, immigration inspectors, criminal investigators, immigration agents, and detention and deportation officers. Nearly half of sworn INS officers are border patrol agents. U.S. Border Patrol agents protect more than eight thousand miles of international land and water boundaries. Their primary mission is to detect and prevent the smuggling and unlawful entry of undocumented aliens into the United States and to apprehend those persons found in violation of the immigration laws. The U.S. Border Patrol is the primary agency monitoring land borders between the ports of entry for illicit drugs and various types of contraband. They accomplish their mission through activities such as tracking, making routine traffic checks on roads and highways leading away from the border, and participating in various task force operations with other law enforcement agencies. Immigration inspectors interview and examine people seeking entrance to the United States and its territories. They inspect passports to determine whether people are legally eligible to enter the United States. Immigration inspectors also prepare reports, maintain records, and process applications and petitions for immigration or temporary residence in the United States.

The federal government maintains a high profile in many areas of law enforcement, with the U.S. Department of Justice serving as the largest employer of sworn federal officers. Federal Bureau of Investigation (FBI) agents are the government's principal investigators, responsible for investigating violations of more than 260 statutes and conducting sensitive national security investigations. Agents may conduct surveillance, monitor court-authorized wiretaps, examine business records, investigate white-collar crime, track the interstate movement of stolen property, collect evidence of espionage activities, or participate in sensitive undercover assignments. The FBI investigates organized crime, public corruption, financial crime, fraud against the government, bribery, copyright infringement, civil rights violations, bank robbery, extortion, kidnapping, air piracy, terrorism, espionage, interstate criminal activity, drug trafficking, and other violations of federal statutes.

Special agents and inspectors employed by the United States Department of the Treasury work for the Bureau of Alcohol, Tobacco, and Firearms (ATF), United States Customs Service, Internal Revenue Service, and United States Secret Service. ATF special agents investigate violations of federal explosives laws, including bombings and arson-for-profit schemes affecting interstate commerce. They may investigate suspected illegal sales, possession, or use of firearms. Other ATF agents investigate violations related to the illegal sale of liquor and interstate smuggling of untaxed cigarettes. These investigations involve surveillance, participation in raids, interviewing suspects, and searching for physical evidence.

Customs agents investigate violations of narcotics smuggling, money laundering, child pornography, customs fraud, and enforcement of the Arms Export Control Act. Domestic and foreign investigations involve the development and use of informants, physical and electronic surveillance, and examination of records from importers/exporters, banks, couriers, and manufacturers. They conduct interviews, serve on joint task forces with other agencies, and obtain and execute search warrants.

Customs inspectors inspect cargo, baggage, and articles worn or carried by people and carriers including vessels, vehicles, trains, and aircraft entering or leaving the United States to enforce laws governing imports and exports. These inspectors examine, count, weigh, gauge, measure, and sample commercial and noncommercial cargoes entering and leaving the United States. Customs inspectors seize prohibited or smuggled articles, intercept contraband, and apprehend, search, detain, and arrest violators of U.S. laws.

Internal Revenue Service special agents collect evidence against individuals and companies that are evading the payment of federal taxes.

U.S. Secret Service agents are charged with two primary missions—protection and investigation. During the course of their careers, they may be assigned to protect the president, vice president, their immediate families, presidential candidates, former presidents, and visiting foreign dignitaries. Secret Service agents also investigate counterfeiting, the forgery of government checks or bonds, and the fraudulent use of credit cards.

Special agents employed by the United States Department of State work for the Diplomatic Security Service. Diplomatic

Security Service special agents advise ambassadors on security matters and manage a complex range of security programs overseas. In the United States, they investigate passport and visa fraud, conduct personnel security investigations, issue security clearances, and protect the secretary of state and certain foreign dignitaries. They train foreign civilian police who then return to their own countries better able to fight terrorism.

Other federal agencies employ police and special agents with sworn arrest powers and the authority to carry firearms. These agencies include the U.S. Postal Service, the Bureau of Indian Affairs Office of Law Enforcement under the U.S. Department of the Interior, the U.S. Forest Service under the U.S. Department of Agriculture, the National Park Service under the U.S. Department of the Interior, and Federal Air Marshals under the U.S. Department of Transportation. Other police agencies have evolved from the need for security for an agency's property and personnel. The largest such agency is the General Services Administration's Federal Protective Service, which provides security for federal workers, buildings, and property. Other examples include the United States Mint police, the Government Printing Service police, and the Central Intelligence Agency's Special Protective Service.

Meet a Special Agent with the FBI

Before becoming a special agent with the Federal Bureau of Investigation, Kevin Illia spent four years in the United States Air Force. After his military service, he went back to school and earned a bachelor's degree from Sonoma State College in California and a master's degree in public affairs from Washington University in St. Louis.

"I was always interested in police and fire fighting and found it natural to take up this career," he said. "When I was in the Air Force serving in a military police unit, we had a warehouse robbery involving about a half a million dollars' worth of stolen equipment. An FBI agent assigned to the case solved it in about two hours, and I was so impressed that I decided this was the career for me."

The follow-up to the story was that the agent surmised the robbery was undoubtedly an "inside job" because the warehouse was isolated on the base. He instructed the military police to gather together all the personnel who worked in that warehouse (a total of ten to fifteen people), and he interviewed them until he was able to elicit a confession from two or three of them. The stolen property was recovered the same night. Case closed.

Illia pointed out that as the largest federal investigative agency in the government, the FBI investigates a wide variety of federal laws. These span everything from bank robbery to kidnappings, civil rights violations, environmental crimes, fair housing infractions, and even violations of the migratory bird act. Anything involving interstate commerce is also in the FBI's jurisdiction. The bureau also covers foreign counterintelligence work, domestic terrorism, and crime on the high seas.

"We train all of our agents to be investigators and that is their primary responsibility, regardless of academic background," he said. "A new agent who comes in as a lawyer or accountant will go through the same sixteen-week training at the FBI Academy at Quantico, Virginia, as a military officer or schoolteacher does. This fact gives continuity to our organization—a common bond of training."

According to Illia, the FBI's application process begins with a detailed screening. Phase one is the written examination, which includes math and English, situational judgment, and cognitive questions. This exam helps in ascertaining whether candidates have analytical skills and common sense so that they are capable of making good choices in a variety of situations. If they pass these tests, they move to an oral assessment interview, where applicants answer questions posed by a board of three special agents. If they pass, they are given drug and polygraph tests. During this step, prospective agents are asked about the veracity of the information they provided in their applications. Typical questions deal with drugs and issues of contact with any foreign intelligence services or terrorist organizations. Those who pass that phase move to the background investigation phase, which covers the applicants' previous ten years. Those applicants who successfully complete all these steps are offered appointments at the FBI Academy as special-agent candidates.

"I'd like to describe what a typical day is like for an FBI agent, but there is no such thing," Illia explained. "Most of the time, the plans you make are disrupted by some event that comes up unexpectedly."

For instance, on one Friday he was prepared to fulfill an obligation to give a presentation to some students. Then a case came up involving a man who had killed two people. Illia was needed to help locate him.

"With search warrant in hand, we scoured his house and found him underneath the bathroom basin," he said. "This was a trick in itself because there were a lot of pipes under the basin and the man was six feet tall. He had his feet wrapped around the pipes somehow, as if he were a contortionist. The point is, you never know what your day will bring."

In considering the qualities that are important for FBI agents, Illia cited flexibility, a desire for adventure, a sense of humor, integrity, perseverance, and tenacity.

"We seek individuals who are interested in making a contribution to their community, their nation, their society," he said. "We want people who are loyal, patriotic, and willing to make sacrifices. It's likely that you'll be relocated to another part of the country and may have to work weekends and sometimes even holidays."

The more skills a potential FBI agent brings to the table, the greater the opportunity for employment, according to Illia. For instance, background as an attorney, accountant, or linguist can be helpful, as can scuba certification, private pilot's licenses, paramedic certification, and/or advanced degrees. The more skills you have, the more valuable you are and the more competitive a candidate you will be. The application process can be lengthy, but for those with patience and the right qualifications, it can lead to an exciting career.

....

Explosives Technicians

Some police officers specialize as explosives technicians. Normally, this means first gaining experience as a police officer, and then completing additional training. Explosives technicians thus must meet the same basic requirements as other police officers. They also earn salaries in the same range as other police officers, although some additional pay for hazardous and/or overtime duty may be earned.

Qualifications and Training Required for Explosives Technicians

An example of the special training needed by explosives technicians is the program offered by the Canadian Police College in Ottawa. Students who complete the Police Explosives Technicians Course (PETC) gain the necessary skills required to render explosives and improvised explosive devices safe. After completing a radiography course, participants study basic explosive theory; identification and safe handling of common commercial explosives; basic knowledge of regulations governing explosives handling, transport, and storage; identification of common military demolition stores and material; rules and regulations governing explosives disposal; initiation and utilization of explosive demolition charges; and other topics.

Students also use of various types of explosives disposal equipment, including robotics (in particular, the remote mobile investigator, or RMI); radiography (x-ray) equipment; hook and line techniques (ropes, hooks, and nets); water gun disruptors; specialized explosive charges; bomb suits and bomb-suit communication devices; and vehicle-opening kits.

Students in these courses must be police personnel who are required to perform the functions of police explosives technicians (PETs). They must also show a willingness to volunteer for PET duties, be recommended after being interviewed by an Explosives Disposal Unit coordinator, have a full understanding of police explosive technician duties, and have five years of experience in the department or experience in related explosives disposal duties, among other requirements.

For more information, contact:

Canadian Police College
P.O. Box 8900
Ottawa, ON K1G 3J2
Canada
www.cpc.gc.ca

Meet an Explosives Technician

Detective Kenneth Rewers gained his experience as an explosives technician and director of the bomb squad with the Cook County Sheriff's Police Department in Illinois. His career began with a job as a patrol officer and was followed by a series of assignments: a task force (a squad put together for problem areas), the detective section (crimes against property), homicide robbery, security detail for the state's attorney, security detail with the sheriff, and running the bomb squad.

"Much of why I'm here today is a result of something that happened one Saturday afternoon when I was working in the detective section out of our Homewood facility," he said. "Someone walked in with a pipe bomb. The desk officer told him that the detectives handle all that, so the man with the bomb walked in and laid it on my desk. I had absolutely no idea what to do, but fortunately there was one police officer on duty who had a military background and some expertise with bombs. We got him in to handle it and that took care of that."

After that incident and a number of others, the department decided that it would be wise to set up a separate bomb unit. Rewers was one of the first to attend the FBI training center in Huntsville, Alabama, where bomb technicians in the United States and from some foreign facilities are trained. The initial training took three-and-a-half weeks. Upon completion, he became certified as an explosives technician. He also completed additional follow-up training.

"Our basic requirement is that you serve five years with the police department first, and then you may apply for an explosives position," Rewers said. "Individuals must realize that it is expensive for the federal government to train individuals for this kind of work and, as a result, you must make a five-year commitment to be a part of one of these units."

According to Rewers, his department's screening procedure for potential newcomers to this field is quite intensive. Candidates must go through several phases of an extensive application and interview process, including an interview that all members of the squad attend.

"The element of trust is so vital that we feel that everyone should share in whether or not a candidate should be accepted," he said.

Once candidates are accepted, they may wait a year or more before having the opportunity to attend school. The training program is attended by about twenty students at a time and is repeated about five or six times a year.

Rewers and his colleagues handle a variety of situations, ranging from bomb cases (typically where teens are experimenting with various types of explosives) to more complex threats. One call from a high school, for instance, resulted when a routine check of student lockers revealed a locker filled with books on how to build explosive devices. The local police called the bomb squad, and the members spoke with the teen who had been using the locker, and then to his parents. It turned out that three explosive devices were in the family's house already, but the parents had no idea of the problem. Thanks to the squad's action, a potential explosion was prevented.

"One important decision we must always make is whether or not to neutralize the devices right on the spot or to move them somewhere else," he said. "You have to evaluate the potential risks involved either or both ways. We do have transporters that help us to move devices; still, you're taking the chance of shaking or disturbing them in trying to move them to a safer place."

Safety is always a major concern, Rewers added. Prompt yet thoughtful decisions must be made. This involves quickly and thoroughly assessing the situation, conferring with one's partner, and deciding the approach to take.

"A mistake can bring tragic results," Rewers said. "You may not get a second chance. But even with that said, and with the danger involved, we who are involved in this career find it to be both interesting and challenging."

Job Settings for Law Enforcement Officers

Law enforcement officers work in a wide range of environments. These may range from city streets or rural highways to desks or offices within police departments.

Police work certainly fits into the "courageous" category. Along with the obvious dangers of confrontations with criminals, police officers must be constantly alert and ready to deal appropriately with a number of other threatening situations. Many law enforcement officers witness death and suffering resulting from accidents and criminal behavior. And a career in law enforcement may take a toll on an officer's private life.

Through the use of government, volunteer, and commercial resources, police are encouraging people in the community to help them identify and solve recurring problems. This involves making the police officer a permanent, highly visible figure in the neighborhood rather than merely an officer called in to respond to a crime.

Regardless of where they work, police officers, detectives, and special agents spend considerable time writing reports and maintaining records. When their arrests result in legal action, they are usually called to testify in court.

Some senior officers, such as chief inspectors, division commanders, division and bureau chiefs, and agents in charge, have additional administrative and supervisory duties. They are often responsible for operation of geographic divisions of an agency, certain kinds of criminal investigations, or various agency functions.

Police officers, detectives, and special agents usually work a forty-hour week, but paid overtime work is common. Several work shifts are necessary since police protection must be provided around the clock. Those with less seniority are most likely to work weekends, holidays, and nights. Police officers, detectives, and special agents are subject to calls at any time their services are needed, and they may work extra-long hours during criminal investigations.

The jobs of some special agents, such as U.S. Secret Service and Drug Enforcement Agency special agents, require extensive travel, often on very short notice. Agents with agencies such as the U.S. Border Patrol have to work outdoors for long periods in all kinds of weather.

While police work is inherently dangerous, good training, teamwork, and equipment such as bullet-resistant vests minimize the number of injuries and fatalities. The risks associated with pursuing speeding motorists, apprehending criminals, and dealing with public disorders can be very stressful for the officers as well as for their families.

Qualifications and Training Required for Law Enforcement Officers

In most states, large municipalities, and special police agencies, civil service regulations govern the appointment of police officers. Candidates must be U.S. citizens, usually at least twenty years of age, and must meet rigorous physical and personal qualifications. In the federal government, candidates must be between twenty-one and thirty-seven years of age at the time of appointment.

Physical examinations for entrance into law enforcement often include tests of vision, hearing, strength, and agility. Eligibility for appointment usually depends on performance in competitive written examinations and previous education and experience. In larger departments, where the majority of law enforcement jobs are found, applicants usually must have at least a high school education. Federal and state agencies usually require college degrees.

Because personal characteristics such as honesty, sound judgment, integrity, and a sense of responsibility are especially important in law enforcement, candidates are interviewed by senior officers, and their character traits and backgrounds are investigated. In some agencies, candidates are interviewed by a psychiatrist or psychologist or given a personality test. Most applicants are subjected to lie detector examinations and drug testing. Some agencies subject sworn personnel to random drug testing as a condition of continuing employment.

Before their first assignments, officers usually go through a period of training. In state and large local departments, recruits get training in their agency's police academy, often for twelve to fourteen weeks. In small agencies, recruits often attend a regional or state academy. Training includes classroom instruction in constitutional law and civil rights, state laws and local ordinances, and accident investigation. Recruits also receive training and supervised experience in patrol, traffic control, use of firearms, self-defense, first aid, and emergency response. Police departments in some cities hire high school graduates still in their teens as cadets or trainees. They do clerical work and attend classes, usually for one to two years, at which point they reach the minimum age requirement and may be appointed to the regular force.

Police officers usually become eligible for promotion after a probationary period ranging from six months to three years. In a large department, promotion may enable an officer to become a detective or specialize in one type of police work, such as working with juveniles. Promotions to corporal, sergeant, lieutenant, and captain usually are made according to a candidate's position on a promotion list, as determined by scores on a written examination and on-the-job performance.

The FBI has the largest number of special agents. To be considered for appointment as an FBI agent, an applicant either must be a graduate of an accredited law school or a college graduate with a major in accounting, fluency in a foreign language, or three years of related full-time work experience. All new agents undergo sixteen weeks of training at the FBI academy on the U.S. Marine Corps base in Quantico, Virginia.

Applicants for special agent jobs with the U.S. Department of Treasury's Secret Service and the Bureau of Alcohol, Tobacco, and Firearms must have bachelor's degrees or a minimum of three years' related work experience. Prospective special agents undergo ten weeks of initial criminal investigation training at the Federal Law Enforcement Training Center in Glynco, Georgia, and another seventeen weeks of specialized training with their particular agencies.

Salaries for Law Enforcement Officers

Police and sheriff's patrol officers had median annual earnings of $39,790 in 2000, according to the U.S. Department of Labor. The middle 50 percent earned between $30,460 and $50,230. The lowest 10 percent earned less than $23,790, and the highest 10 percent earned more than $58,900. Median annual earnings were $44,400 in state government, $39,710 in local government, and $37,760 in the federal government.

Median annual earnings of police and detective supervisors were $57,210 in 2000. The middle 50 percent earned between $43,630 and $70,680. The lowest 10 percent earned less than $34,660, and the highest 10 percent earned more than $86,060.

Median annual earnings for law enforcement professionals in the federal government were $74,070, $57,030 in local government, and $53,960 in state government.

In 2000, median annual earnings of detectives and criminal investigators were $48,870. The middle 50 percent earned between $37,240 and $61,750. The lowest 10 percent earned less than $29,600, and the highest 10 percent earned more than $72,160. Median annual earnings were $61,180 in the federal government, $46,340 in local government, and $43,050 in state government.

Federal law provides special salary rates to federal employees who serve in law enforcement. Additionally, federal special agents and inspectors receive law enforcement availability pay (LEAP)—equal to 25 percent of the agent's grade and step—awarded because of the large amount of overtime that these agents are expected to work. For example, in 2001 FBI agents entered federal service as GS-10 employees on the pay scale at a base salary of $36,621, yet they earned about $45,776 a year with availability pay. They could advance to the GS-13 grade level in field non-supervisory assignments at a base salary of $57,345, or $71,681 with availability pay.

FBI supervisory, management, and executive positions in grades GS-14 and GS-15 paid a base salary between $67,765 and $79,710 a year, respectively, and equaled $84,706 or $99,637 per year including availability pay. Salaries were slightly higher in selected areas where the prevailing local pay level was higher. Because federal agents may be eligible for a special law enforcement benefits package, applicants should ask their recruiters for more information.

For Additional Information

American Society for Law Enforcement Training
121 North Court Street
Frederick, MD 21701
www.aslet.org

International Crime Scene Investigators Association (ICSIA)
PMB 385
15774 South LaGrange Road
Orland Park, IL 60462
www.icsia.com

International Police Association, Canadian Section
Secretary General, IPA Canada
P.O. Box 882
Coalhurst, AB T0L 0V0
Canada
www.ipa.ca

National Black Police Association
3251 Mt. Pleasant Street NW, Second Floor
Washington, DC 20010
www.blackpolice.org

National Police and Security Officers Association of America
P.O. Box 663
South Plainfield, NJ 07080
http://npoaa.tripod.com

National Sheriffs' Association
1450 Duke Street
Alexandria, VA 22314
www.sheriffs.org

United States Deputy Sheriffs' Association
1304 Langham Creek Drive, Suite 324
Houston, TX 77084
www.usdsa.org

United States Marshals Service
Human Resources Division
Law Enforcement Recruiting
Washington, DC 20530
www.usdoj.gov/marshals

················

Guards

Guards (sometimes called security officers) patrol and inspect property to protect against fire, theft, vandalism, and illegal entry. Their duties vary with the size, type, and location of the employer. Most large organizations, whether they are businesses or non-profit enterprises, employ security guards or contract for their services, as do some smaller ones.

Zeroing in on What a Guard Does

In office buildings, banks, hospitals, and department stores, guards protect records, merchandise, money, and equipment. In department stores, they often work with undercover detectives to watch for theft by customers or store employees. Some guards patrol the outside of these buildings.

At ports, airports, and railroads, guards protect merchandise being shipped as well as property and equipment. They screen passengers and visitors for weapons, explosives, and other contraband. They ensure that nothing is stolen while being loaded or unloaded, and they watch for fires, prowlers, and trouble among work crews. Sometimes they direct traffic.

Guards who work in public buildings, such as museums or art galleries, protect paintings and exhibits by inspecting people and packages entering the building. They also answer routine questions from visitors and sometimes guide tours.

In factories, laboratories, government buildings, data processing centers, and military bases where valuable property or information—such as information on new products, computer codes, or defense secrets—must be protected, guards check the credentials of persons and vehicles entering and leaving the premises. University, park, or recreation guards perform similar duties and also may issue parking permits and direct traffic. Those who patrol golf courses prevent unauthorized persons from using the facilities and help keep play running smoothly.

At social affairs, sports events, conventions, and other public gatherings, guards provide information, assist in crowd control, and watch for persons who may cause trouble. Some guards patrol places of entertainment, such as nightclubs, to preserve order among customers and to protect property. Armored car guards protect money and valuables during transit.

In a large organization, a security officer often is in charge of the guard force; in a small organization, a single worker may be responsible for all security measures. Patrolling usually is done on foot, but if the property is large, guards may make their rounds by car or motor scooter. As more businesses make use of advanced electronic security systems to protect their property, more guards are being assigned to stations where they monitor perimeter security, environmental functions, communications, and other systems. In many cases, these guards maintain radio contact with other guards who are patrolling on foot or in motor vehicles. Some guards use computers to store information on matters relevant to security, such as suspicious visitors or occurrences during their hours on duty.

As they make their rounds, guards check all doors and windows, see that no unauthorized persons remain after working hours, and ensure that fire extinguishers, alarms, sprinkler systems, furnaces, and various electrical and plumbing systems are working properly. They sometimes set thermostats or turn on lights for janitorial workers.

Although some guards carry weapons, many employers prefer not to use armed guards. Guards may also carry flashlights, whistles, two-way radios, and watch clocks, devices that indicate the time at which the guards reach various checkpoints.

Most guards spend considerable time on their feet patrolling buildings, industrial plants, and grounds. Indoors, they may be stationed at a guard desk to monitor electronic security and surveillance devices or to check the credentials of persons entering or leaving the premises. They also may be stationed at gate shelters or may patrol grounds in all weather.

Because guards often work alone, there may be no one nearby to help if an accident or injury occurs. Some large firms use a reporting service that enables guards to be in constant contact with a central station outside the plant. If they fail to transmit an expected signal, the central station investigates.

Guard work is usually somewhat routine, but guards must be constantly alert for threats to themselves and to the property that they are protecting. Guards who work during the day may have a great deal of contact with other employees and members of the public.

Many guards work alone at night. The usual shift lasts eight hours. Some employers run three shifts, and guards rotate to divide daytime, weekend, and holiday work equally. Guards generally eat on the job instead of taking a regular break away from the site.

Qualifications and Training Required for Guards

Most states require that guards be licensed. To be licensed as a guard, individuals generally must be at least eighteen years old, have no police record or convictions for perjury or acts of violence, pass a background examination, and complete classroom training in such subjects as property rights, emergency procedures, and seizure of suspected criminals.

Most employers prefer guards who are high school graduates. Some jobs require a driver's license. Employers also seek people who have had experience in the military police or in state and local police departments. Most persons entering guard jobs have prior work experience, although it is usually unrelated. Because of limited formal training requirements and flexible hours, this occupation attracts some persons seeking a second job. For some entrants, such as those retired from military careers or other protective services, guard employment is a second career.

Applicants are expected to have positive character references, good health (especially in hearing and vision), and good personal habits, such as neatness and dependability. In order to cope with emergencies, they should be mentally alert, emotionally stable, and physically fit. Guards who have frequent contact with the public should be friendly and personable. Some employers require applicants to take a polygraph examination or a written test of honesty, attitudes, and other personal qualities. Employers may require applicants and experienced workers to submit to drug screening tests as a condition of employment.

Candidates for guard jobs in the federal government must have some experience as a guard and pass a written examination. Armed forces experience also is an asset. For most federal guard positions, applicants must qualify in the use of firearms.

The amount of training guards receive varies. Training requirements generally are increasing as modern, highly sophisticated security systems become more commonplace. Many employers give newly hired guards instruction before they start the job and also provide several weeks of on-the-job training.

A number of states have made ongoing training a legal requirement. For example, New York now requires guards to complete forty hours of training after starting work. Illinois requires twenty hours for unarmed guards, plus an additional twenty hours for armed guards. Guards receive training in protection, public relations, report writing, crisis deterrence, first aid, and drug control, as well as specialized training relevant to their particular assignments. Guards employed at establishments that place a heavy emphasis on security usually receive extensive formal training. For example, guards at nuclear power plants may undergo several months of training before being placed on duty under close supervision. Guards may be taught to use firearms, administer first aid, operate alarm systems and electronic security equipment, and spot and deal with security problems. Guards who are authorized to carry firearms may be tested periodically in their use according to state or local laws. Some guards are tested periodically for strength and endurance.

Although guards in small companies receive periodic salary increases, advancement is likely to be limited. However, most large organizations use a military type of ranking that offers advancement in position and salary. Higher-level guard experience may enable persons to transfer to police jobs that offer higher pay and greater opportunities for advancement. Guards with some college education may advance to jobs that involve administrative and management duties. A few guards with management skills open their own contract security guard agencies.

Job Settings for Guards

Industrial security firms and guard agencies employ the majority of guards. These organizations provide security services on contract, assigning their guards to buildings and other sites as needed. The remainder are in-house guards, employed in many settings, including banks, building management companies, hotels, hospitals, retail stores, restaurants and bars, schools, and government operations.

Although guard jobs are found throughout the country, most are located in metropolitan areas. Guards employed by industrial security companies and guard agencies are occasionally laid off when the firms at which they work do not renew contract with their agencies. Most are able to find employment with other agencies, however. Guards who are employed directly by the firms at which they work are seldom laid off because a plant or factory must still be protected even when economic conditions force it to close temporarily.

Information about work opportunities for guards is available from local detective and guard firms and the nearest state employment service office. Information about licensing requirements for guards may be obtained from the state licensing commission or the state police department. In states where local jurisdictions establish licensing requirements, contact a local government authority such as the sheriff, county executive, or city manager.

Salaries for Guards

According to the U.S. Department of Labor, median annual earnings of security guards were $17,570 in 2000. The middle 50 percent earned between $14,930 and $21,950. The lowest 10 percent earned less than $12,860, and the highest 10 percent earned more than $28,660. The industries employing the largest numbers of security guards in 2000 were hospitals, elementary and secondary schools, hotels and motels, and miscellaneous business services.

Depending on their experience, newly hired guards in the federal government earned $21,950 to $27,190 a year in 2001. Beginning salaries were slightly higher in selected areas where the prevailing local pay level was higher. Guards employed by the federal government averaged $28,960 a year in 2001. These workers usually receive overtime pay as well as a wage differential for the second and third shifts.

Correctional Officers

Correctional officers are charged with overseeing individuals who have been arrested, are awaiting trial or hearing, or have been convicted of a crime and sentenced to serve time in a jail, reformatory, or penitentiary. They maintain security and observe inmate conduct and behavior to prevent disturbances and escapes.

Zeroing in on What a Correctional Officer Does

Many correctional officers work in small county and municipal jails or precinct station houses as deputy sheriffs or police officers with wide-ranging responsibilities. Others are assigned to large state and federal prisons where job duties are more specialized. A relatively small number supervise aliens being held by the Immigration and Naturalization Service before being released or deported. Regardless of the setting, correctional officers maintain order within the institution, enforce rules and regulations, and may supplement whatever counseling inmates receive from psychologists, social workers, or other mental health professionals.

To make sure inmates are orderly and obey rules, correctional officers monitor inmates' activities, including working, exercising, eating, and bathing. They supervise inmates' work assignments. Sometimes it is necessary to search inmates and their living quarters for weapons or drugs, to settle disputes between inmates, and to enforce discipline. Correctional officers cannot show favoritism and must report any inmate who violates the rules. Officers responsible for direct supervision of inmates are unarmed. They are locked in a cell block (alone or with another officer) among the fifty to one hundred inmates who reside there. The officers enforce regulations primarily through their communications skills and moral authority. A few officers hold staff security positions in towers, where they are equipped with high-powered rifles.

Other correctional officers periodically inspect the facilities. They may check cells and other areas of the institution for unsanitary conditions, weapons, drugs, fire hazards, and any evidence of rules infractions. In addition, they routinely inspect locks, window bars, grille doors, and gates for signs of tampering.

Correctional officers report orally and in writing on inmate conduct and the quality and quantity of work done by inmates. Officers also report disturbances, violations of rules, and any unusual occurrences. They usually keep a daily record of their activities. In the most modern facilities, correctional officers can monitor the activities of prisoners from a centralized control center with the aid of closed-circuit television cameras and a computer tracking system. In such an environment, the inmates may not see anyone but officers for days or weeks at a time.

Depending on the offenders' classifications within the institution, correctional officers may escort inmates to and from cells and other areas and admit and accompany authorized visitors to see inmates. Officers may also escort prisoners between the institution and courtrooms, medical facilities, and other destinations. They inspect mail and visitors for contraband (prohibited items). Should the situation arise, they assist law enforcement authorities by investigating crimes committed within their institutions and by helping search for escaped inmates.

Correctional officers may help inmates get news of their families, arrange a daily schedule change so that an inmate can visit the library, or help inmates in other ways. In a few institutions, officers receive specialized training, have more formal counseling roles, and may lead or participate in group counseling sessions.

Correctional sergeants directly supervise correctional officers and are responsible for the safety and well being of the individuals in their keeping. They usually are responsible for maintaining security and directing the activities of a group of inmates during an assigned watch or in an assigned area.

Correctional officers may work indoors or outdoors, depending on their specific duties. Some indoor areas in these facilities are well lighted, heated, and ventilated, but others are overcrowded, hot, and noisy. Outdoors, weather conditions may be disagreeable, such as when standing watch in a guard tower in cold weather. Working in a correctional institution can be stressful and hazardous; correctional officers occasionally have been injured or killed by inmates.

Correctional officers usually work eight-hour days, five days a week, on rotating shifts. Prison security must be provided around the clock, which means junior officers work weekends, holidays, and nights. Officers also may be required to work overtime.

Qualifications and Training Required for Correctional Officers

Most institutions require correctional officers to be at least eighteen or twenty-one years of age, have a high school education or equivalent, have no felony convictions, and be a United States citizen. In addition, institutions increasingly seek correctional officers with post-secondary education, particularly in psychology, criminal justice, police science, criminology, and related fields.

Correctional officers must be in good health. The federal system and many states require candidates to meet formal standards of physical fitness, eyesight, and hearing. Strength, good judgment, and the ability to think and act quickly are indispensable. Other common requirements include a driver's license and work experience that demonstrates reliability. Applicants are usually screened for drug abuse, and candidates must pass a written or oral examination, along with a background check.

Federal, state, and local corrections departments provide training for correctional officers based on guidelines established by the American Correctional Association, the American Jail Association, and other professional organizations. Some states have special training academies. All state and local corrections departments provide on-the-job training at the end of formal instruction. On-the-job trainees receive several weeks or months of training in actual job settings under experienced officers.

Academy trainees generally receive instruction on institutional policies, regulations, and operations; constitutional law and cultural awareness; crisis intervention, inmate behavior, and contraband control; custody and security procedures; fire and safety; inmate rules and legal rights; administrative responsibilities; written and oral communication, including preparation of reports; self-defense, including the use of firearms and physical force; first aid, including cardiopulmonary resuscitation (CPR); and physical fitness training. New federal correctional officers must undergo two hundred hours of formal training within the first year of employment. They must complete 120 hours of correctional instruction at the Federal Bureau of Prisons residential training center at Glynco, Georgia, within the first sixty days after appointment. Experienced officers receive in-service training to keep abreast of new ideas and procedures.

Entry requirements and on-the-job training vary widely from agency to agency. For instance, correctional officers in North Dakota need two years of college with emphasis on criminal justice or behavioral science, or three years as a correctional, military police, or licensed peace officer. The department then provides eighty hours of training at the start and follows with forty hours of training annually. On the other hand, Connecticut requires only that candidates be eighteen years of age, have a high school diploma or GED certificate, and pass medical and physical examinations, including drug screening. It then provides 520 hours of initial training and follows with 40 hours annually.

Correctional officers have the opportunity to join prison tactical response teams, which are trained to respond to riots, hostage situations, forced cell moves, and other potentially dangerous confrontations. Team members often receive monthly training and practice with weapons, chemical agents, forced-entry methods, and other tactics.

With education, experience, and training, qualified officers may advance to correctional sergeant or other supervisory or administrative positions. Many correctional institutions require experience as a correctional officer for other corrections positions. Ambitious correctional officers can be promoted to assistant warden or warden. Officers sometimes transfer to related areas, such as probation or parole officer.

Job Settings for Correctional Officers

About six of every ten correctional officers work at state correctional institutions such as prisons, prison camps, and reformatories. Most of the remainder work at city and county jails or other institutions run by local governments. About nine thousand correctional officers work at federal correctional institutions, and approximately four thousand work in privately owned and managed prisons.

Some 118 jail systems housing more than a thousand prisoners are located in urban areas, though most correctional officers work in institutions located in rural areas with smaller inmate populations. A significant number work in jails and other facilities that are located in law enforcement agencies throughout the country.

Salaries for Correctional Officers

According to the U.S. Department of Labor, median annual earnings of correctional officers were $31,170 in 2000. The middle 50 percent earned between $24,650 and $40,100. The lowest 10 percent earned less than $20,010, and the highest 10 percent earned more than $49,310. Median annual earnings were $37,430 in the federal government, $31,860 in state government, and $29,240 in local government. In the management and public relations industry, where officers employed by privately operated prisons are classified, median annual earnings were $21,600. According to the Federal Bureau of Prisons, the starting salary for federal correctional officers was about $27,000 a year in 2001. Starting federal salaries were slightly higher in selected areas where prevailing local pay levels were higher.

Median annual earnings of first-line supervisors or managers of correctional officers were $41,880 in 2000. The middle 50 percent earned between $32,460 and $55,540; the lowest 10 percent earned less than $28,280, and the highest 10 percent earned more than $67,280. Median annual earnings were $40,560 in state government and $49,680 in local government.

For Additional Information

Information about entrance requirements, training, and career opportunities for correctional officers on the state level may be obtained from state civil service commissions, state departments of corrections, nearby correctional institutions and facilities, and the following professional associations.

The American Jail Association
1135 Professional Court
Hagerstown, MD 21740
www.corrections.com/aja

American Correctional Association
4380 Forbes Boulevard
Lanham, MD 20706
www.aca.org
g
Correctional Service of Canada
National Headquarters
Human Resources Division
340 Laurier Avenue West
Ottawa, ON K1A 0P9
Canada
www.csc-scc.gc.ca

Information on entrance requirements, training, and career opportunities for correctional officers on the federal level may be obtained from:

Federal Bureau of Prisons
National Recruitment Office
320 First Street NW, Room 460
Washington, DC 20534
www.bop.gov

CHAPTER SIX

Careers for Other Courageous Spirits

The brave man is not he who feels no fear,
For that were stupid and irrational;
But he, whose noble soul its fears subdues,
And bravely dares the danger nature shrinks from.
—Joanna Baillie, "Basil: A Tragedy"

Throughout this book, you've read profiles of a variety of jobs requiring an extra bit of courage or adding an element of excitement not found in more mundane occupations. But keep in mind that there are many more jobs out there that might appeal to courageous types. Here is an overview of some of them.

Firefighters

The first fire departments were neighbors who got together in times of crisis to help one another. "Bucket brigades" were formed to connect the closest sources of water to the scene of the fire. By the turn of the century, most local municipalities had created their own professional fire departments. Since that time, highly organized fire departments have become a central part of the infrastructure that protects our society.

Zeroing in on What a Firefighter Does

Firefighters respond to a variety of emergency situations in which life, property, or the environment is at risk. Frequently, they are the first emergency response personnel to arrive at the scene of an accident, fire, flood, earthquake, or act of terrorism. Who can forget the dramatic stories of the roles played by firefighters during the 2001 destruction of the World Trade Center buildings in New York City? Every year, fires and other emergency conditions take thousands of lives and destroy property worth billions of dollars. Firefighters help protect the public against these dangers, whether they are career firefighters or volunteers who serve with no pay.

Firefighting is a potentially hazardous occupation. Injuries can result from smoke inhalation, flames, and walls and floors giving way as a result of the fire. Exposure to hazardous materials is also a possibility, even with the protective gear firefighters wear.

Most calls that firefighters respond to involve emergencies of a medical nature, and many fire departments provide ambulance service for victims. Firefighters receive training in emergency medical procedures, and fire departments often require them to be certified as emergency medical technicians.

When on duty, firefighters must always be prepared to respond immediately to a fire or other emergency situation that arises. Because fire fighting is dangerous and complicated, it requires organization and teamwork. At each emergency scene, firefighters are assigned specific duties by a superior officer. This could be connecting hose lines to hydrants, positioning ladders, or operating pumps. Firefighters may rescue victims and administer emergency medical aid, ventilate smoke-filled areas, operate equipment, and salvage the contents of buildings. Their duties may change several times while the company is in action. Sometimes they remain at the site of a disaster for several days or more, rescuing survivors and assisting with medical emergencies.

A firefighter's responsibilities have become more complex in recent years due to the use of increasingly sophisticated equipment. In addition, many firefighters have assumed a wider range of responsibilities. For example, they may find themselves assisting in recovery from natural disasters such as earthquakes and tornadoes or becoming involved with the control and cleanup of oil spills or other hazardous materials incidents.

Firefighters are primarily involved with protecting structures, but they also work at airports, at chemical plants, on crash and rescue crews, near waterfronts, and in forests and wildland areas. In forests, air patrols locate fires and report their findings to headquarters by telephone or radio. Fire rangers patrol areas of the forest to locate and report fires and hazardous conditions and to ensure that travelers and campers are complying with fire regulations. When fires break out in the forest, firefighters use hand tools and water hoses to battle the blaze. When necessary, specialized firefighters parachute from airplanes in order to reach inaccessible areas.

Most fire departments are headed by a fire marshal who is in charge of the fire prevention division. Fire inspectors are specially trained to conduct inspections of structures and to ensure fire code compliance in order to prevent fires. They may also check and approve plans for new buildings, working with developers and planners in the process. Fire prevention personnel often speak on these subjects before public assemblies and civic organizations.

Some firefighters become fire investigators, who determine the origin and cause of fires. They collect evidence, interview witnesses, and prepare reports on fires that may involve arson or criminal negligence. Some investigators even have the power of police officers, with authority to arrest suspects and testify in court.

Between alarms, firefighters are required to attend classes, clean and maintain equipment, conduct practice drills and fire inspections, and participate in physical fitness activities. They prepare written reports on fire incidents and review fire science literature to keep abreast of technological developments and administrative practices and policies.

Firefighters spend much of their time at fire stations, which usually have facilities for dining and sleeping. When an alarm comes in, firefighters must respond rapidly, regardless of the weather or hour. They may spend arduous periods on their feet, sometimes in adverse weather.

Firefighters often work long hours—perhaps more than fifty hours a week. In some cities, they are on duty for twenty-four hours, then off for forty-eight hours, receiving an extra day off at regular intervals. In other cities, they work a day shift of ten hours for three or four days, a night shift of fourteen hours for three or four nights, then have three or four days off, and then repeat the cycle. In addition, firefighters often work extra hours at fires and other emergencies and are regularly assigned to work on holidays. Fire lieutenants and fire captains often work the same hours as the firefighters they supervise. Shift hours include time when firefighters study, train, and perform fire prevention duties.

Qualifications and Training Required for Firefighters

Candidates for municipal fire fighting jobs may be required to pass written examinations; tests of strength, physical stamina, coordination, and agility; and a medical examination that includes drug screening. (Once on the job, workers may be monitored for drug use on a random basis.) In some departments, examinations are open to persons between eighteen and thirty-one years of age who have a high school education or the equivalent. Those who receive the highest scores and those who have completed community college courses in fire science have the best chances for appointment. In recent years, an increasing proportion of entrants to this occupation have some postsecondary education to their credit.

Usually, beginners in large fire departments are trained for several weeks at the department's training center or in state training programs. Through classroom instruction and practical training, the recruits study fire fighting techniques, fire prevention, hazardous materials, local building codes, and emergency medical procedures, including first aid and cardiopulmonary resuscitation. Also, they learn how to use axes, saws, chemical extinguishers, ladders, and other fire fighting and rescue equipment. After successfully completing this training, they are assigned to a fire company, where they undergo a period of probation.

A number of fire departments have accredited three- or four-year apprenticeship programs. These programs combine formal, technical instruction with on-the-job training under the supervision of experienced firefighters. Technical instruction covers subjects such as emergency medical procedures, fire fighting techniques and equipment, fire prevention and safety, and chemical hazards associated with various combustible building materials.

To improve their job performance and prepare for examinations, most experienced firefighters continue studying. Today, firefighters need more training to operate increasingly sophisticated equipment and to deal safely with the greater hazards associated with fighting fires in larger, more elaborate structures. To progress to higher-level positions, they must acquire expertise in the most advanced fire fighting equipment and techniques and in building construction, emergency medical procedures, writing, public speaking, management, budgeting procedures, and labor relations. Fire departments frequently conduct training programs, and some firefighters attend training sessions sponsored by the National Fire Academy. These training sessions cover various topics, including executive development, anti-arson techniques, and public fire safety and education.

Many colleges and universities offer courses leading to two- or four-year degrees in fire engineering or fire science. Many fire departments offer firefighters incentives such as tuition reimbursement or higher pay for completing advanced training. Firefighters stay abreast of technology developments and new techniques in the profession through conferences, seminars, and workshops.

Desirable qualities for firefighters include endurance, courage, mental alertness, a sense of public service, proficient communication skills, mechanical aptitude, and strength. Initiative and good judgment are extremely important because firefighters often must make quick decisions in emergencies. Because members of a crew eat, sleep, and work closely together under conditions of stress and danger, they should be dependable and able to get along well with others in a group. Leadership qualities are necessary for officers, who must establish and maintain discipline and efficiency as well as direct the activities of firefighters in their companies.

Opportunities for promotion are good in most fire departments. As firefighters gain experience, they may advance to higher ranks. Generally, the line of promotion, in ascending order, is from firefighter to:

- engineer
- lieutenant
- captain
- battalion chief
- assistant chief
- deputy chief
- chief

Advancement generally depends upon scores on a written examination, job performance, and seniority. Increasingly, fire departments are using assessment centers that simulate a variety of actual job performance tasks to screen for the best candidates for promotion. Many fire departments now require a bachelor's degree, preferably in public administration or a related field, for promotion to positions higher than battalion chief. Some departments now require a master's degree for the chief or for a state chief officer certification. The National Fire Academy requires a master's degree for executive fire officer certification.

Job Settings for Firefighters
According to the U.S. Department of Labor, paid career firefighters held about 258,000 jobs in 2000. First-line supervisors and managers of fire fighting and prevention workers held about

sixty-two thousand jobs, and fire inspectors held about thirteen thousand. More than nine out of ten worked in municipal or county fire departments. Some large cities have thousands of career firefighters, while many small towns have only a few. Most of the remainder work in fire departments on federal and state installations, including airports. Private fire fighting companies employ a small number of firefighters and usually operate on a subscription basis.

In response to the expanding role of firefighters, some municipalities have combined fire prevention, public fire education, safety, and emergency medical services into a single organization commonly referred to as a public safety organization. Some local and regional fire departments are being consolidated into countywide establishments in order to reduce administrative staffs and cut costs and to establish consistent training standards and work procedures.

Salaries of Firefighters

According to the U.S. Department of Labor, median hourly earnings of firefighters were $16.43 in 2000. The middle 50 percent earned between $11.82 and $21.75. The lowest 10 percent earned less than $8.03, and the highest 10 percent earned more than $26.58. Median hourly earnings were $16.71 in local government and $15.00 in the federal government.

Median annual earnings of first-line supervisors or managers of fire fighting and prevention workers were $51,990 in 2000. The middle 50 percent earned between $40,920 and $64,760. The lowest 10 percent earned less than $31,820, and the highest 10 percent earned more than $77,700. First-line supervisors or managers of fire fighting and prevention workers employed in local government earned about $52,390 a year in 2000.

Median annual earnings of fire inspectors and investigators were $41,630 in 2000. The middle 50 percent earned between $31,630 and $53,130 a year. The lowest 10 percent earned less than $24,790, and the highest 10 percent earned more than $65,030.

Fire inspectors and investigators employed in local government earned about $44,030 a year in 2000.

Median annual earnings of forest fire inspectors and prevention specialists were $32,140 in 2000. The middle 50 percent earned between $22,930 and $41,150 a year. The lowest 10 percent earned less than $17,060, and the highest 10 percent earned more than $50,680.

For Additional Information

International Association of Firefighters
1750 New York Avenue NW
Washington, DC 20006
www.iaff.org

International Association of Fire Chiefs
4025 Fair Ridge Drive
Fairfax, VA 22033
www.ichiefs.org

National Association of Hispanic Firefighters
2821 McKinney Avenue, Suite 7
Dallas, TX 75204
www.nahf.org

National Fire Academy
16825 South Seton Avenue
Emmitsburg, MD 21727
www.usfa.fema.gov/fire-service/nfa/nfa.shtm

U.S. Fire Administration
16825 South Seton Avenue
Emmitsburg, MD 21727
www.usfa.fema.gov

Emergency Medical Technicians

Another career possibility for courageous people is that of the emergency medical technician (EMT). Sometimes firefighters may act as both emergency medical technicians and as firefighters, and sometimes these are separate roles. In either case, the work involved provides a badly needed service while also offering some exciting career possibilities.

Zeroing in on What an EMT Does

Automobile accident injuries, heart attacks, near drownings, unscheduled childbirths, poisonings, and gunshot wounds all demand urgent medical attention. Emergency medical technicians (EMTs) and paramedics (EMTs with additional advanced training to perform more difficult prehospital medical procedures) are the ones who provide that immediate care and then transport the sick or injured to medical facilities.

Following instructions from a dispatcher, EMTs (who usually work in pairs in specially equipped vehicles) are called to an emergency scene. If necessary, they request additional help from police or fire department personnel. They determine the nature and extent of the patient's injuries or illness while also trying to determine whether the patient has epilepsy, diabetes, or other preexisting medical conditions. EMTs then give appropriate emergency care based upon the strict guidelines that dictate the procedures they may perform. All EMTs, including those with basic skills (the EMT-Basic) may open airways, restore breathing, control bleeding, treat for shock, administer oxygen, immobilize fractures, bandage wounds, assist in childbirth, manage emotionally disturbed patients, treat and assist heart attack victims, give initial care to poison and burn victims, and treat patients with antishock trousers (which prevent a person's blood pressure from falling too low).

EMT-Intermediates (or EMT-Is) have more advanced training that allows them to administer intravenous fluids, use defibrillators to give lifesaving shocks to a stopped heart, and handle other intensive care procedures.

EMT-Paramedics (or EMT-Ps) provide the most extensive prehospital care. In addition to the procedures already described, paramedics may administer drugs either intravenously or orally, interpret electrocardiograms (EKGs), and use monitors and other complex equipment.

When victims are trapped, as in the case of an automobile accident, cave-in, or building collapse, EMTs free them or provide emergency care while others free them. Some conditions are simple enough to be handled by following general rules and guidelines. More complicated problems can only be carried out under the step-by-step direction of medical personnel by radio contact.

When transporting patients to a medical facility, EMTs may use special equipment such as backboards to immobilize patients before placing them on stretchers and securing them in the ambulance. While one EMT drives, the other monitors the patient's vital signs and gives additional care as needed.

At the medical facility, EMTs transfer patients to the emergency department, report to the staff their observations and the care they provided, and help provide emergency treatment. In rural areas, some EMT-Ps are trained to treat patients with minor injuries on the scene of an accident or at their home without transporting them to a medical facility.

After each run, EMTs replace used supplies and check equipment. If patients have had a contagious disease, EMTs decontaminate the interior of the ambulance and report cases to the proper authorities.

EMTs work both indoors and outdoors in all kinds of weather. Much of their time is spent standing, kneeling, bending, and lifting. They may risk noise-induced hearing loss from ambulance sirens and back injuries from lifting patients. EMTs may be exposed to diseases such as Hepatitis-B and AIDS, as well as violence from individuals suffering with drug overdoses or those who are too sick to be cognizant of their actions. Not surprisingly, the work is not only physically strenuous, but stressful.

EMTs employed by fire departments often have about a fifty-hour work week. Those employed by hospitals frequently work between forty-five and fifty-eight hours a week, and those in private ambulance services between forty-eight and fifty-one hours. Some EMTs, especially those in police and fire departments, are on call for extended periods. Because most emergency services function twenty-four hours a day, EMTs have irregular working hours that add to job stress.

Despite the difficult working conditions, many emergency medical technicians find their work exciting and challenging.

Qualifications and Training Required for EMTs

Formal training and certification are needed to become an EMT or paramedic. According to the U.S. Department of Labor, all fifty states have certification procedures. In thirty-eight states and the District of Columbia, registration with the National Registry of Emergency Medical Technicians (NREMT) is required at some or all levels of certification. Other states administer their own certification examinations or provide the option of taking the NREMT examination. To maintain certification, EMTs and paramedics must reregister, usually every two years. In order to reregister, an individual must be working as an EMT or paramedic and meet a continuing education requirement.

Training is offered at progressive levels: EMT-Basic, also known as EMT-1; EMT-Intermediate, or EMT-2 and EMT-3; and EMT-Paramedic, or EMT-4. The EMT-Basic represents the first level of skills required to work in the emergency medical system. Course work typically emphasizes emergency skills such as managing respiratory, trauma, and cardiac emergencies and patient assessment.

Formal courses are often combined with time in an emergency room or ambulance. The program also provides instruction and practice in dealing with bleeding, fractures, airway obstruction, cardiac arrest, and emergency childbirth. Students learn to use and maintain common emergency equipment, such as backboards, suction devices, splints, oxygen delivery systems, and stretchers. Graduates of approved EMT-Basic training programs who pass a written and practical examination administered by the state certifying agency or the NREMT earn the title of Registered EMT-Basic. The course is a prerequisite for EMT-Intermediate and EMT-Paramedic training as well.

EMT-Intermediate training requirements vary from state to state. Applicants can opt to receive training in EMT-Shock Trauma, where the caregiver learns to start intravenous fluids and give certain medications, or in EMT-Cardiac, which includes learning heart rhythms and administering advanced medications. Training commonly includes thirty-five to fifty-five hours of additional instruction beyond EMT-Basic course work and covers patient assessment as well as the use of advanced airway devices and intravenous fluids. Prerequisites for the EMT-Intermediate examination include registration as an EMT-Basic, required classroom work, and a specified amount of clinical experience.

The most advanced level of training for this occupation is EMT-Paramedic. At this level, the caregiver receives additional training in body function and more advanced skills. The Paramedic Technology program usually lasts up to two years and results in an associate's degree in applied science. Such education prepares the graduate to take the NREMT examination and become certified as an EMT-Paramedic. Extensive related course work and clinical and field experience are required. Refresher courses and continuing education are available for EMTs and paramedics at all levels.

EMTs and paramedics should be emotionally stable; have good dexterity, agility, and physical coordination; and be able to lift and carry heavy loads. They also need good eyesight (corrective lenses may be used) with accurate color vision.

Job Settings for EMTs

About two-fifths of EMTs serve in private ambulance services; about one-third are in municipal fire, police, or rescue squad departments; and one-fourth serve in hospitals. In addition, many EMTs are volunteers. Most career EMTs work in metropolitan areas. Smaller towns often don't have the funds to employ EMTs.

In the near future, most opportunities for EMTs and paramedics are expected to arise in hospitals and private ambulance services. Competition will be greater for jobs in local government, including fire, police, and independent rescue squad departments, where salaries and benefits tend to be slightly better. Opportunities will be best for those who have advanced certifications, such as EMT-Intermediate and EMT-Paramedic, as clients and patients demand higher levels of care before arriving at the hospital.

Salaries for EMTs

Salaries or wages for EMTs and paramedics depend on the employment setting and geographic location as well as the individual's training and experience. Median annual earnings of EMTs and paramedics were $22,460 in 2000, according to the U.S. Department of Labor. The middle 50 percent earned between $17,930 and $29,270. The lowest 10 percent earned less than $14,660, and the highest 10 percent earned more than $37,760.

Median annual earnings in the industries employing the largest numbers of EMTs and paramedics in 2000 were $24,800 in local government, $23,590 in hospitals, and $20,950 in local and suburban transportation. Those in emergency medical services who are part of fire or police departments receive the same benefits as firefighters or police officers. For example, many are covered by pension plans that provide retirement at half pay after twenty or twenty-five years of service or if disabled in the line of duty.

For Additional Information

Information concerning training courses, registration, and job opportunities for EMTs can be obtained by writing to the state Emergency Medical Service Director and from the following professional associations.

National Association of Emergency Medical Technicians
(NAEMT)
P.O. Box 1400
Clinton, MS 39060
www.naemt.org

National Registry of Emergency Medical Technicians
P.O. Box 29233
Columbus, OH 43229
www.nremt.org

National Highway Transportation Safety Administration
Emergency Medical Services Division
400 Seventh Street SW, NTS-14
Washington, DC 20590
www.nhtsa.dot.gov/people/injury/ems

Paramedic Association of Canada
300 March Road, Fourth Floor
Ottawa, ON K2K 2E2
Canada
www.paramedic.ca

Private Detectives and Investigators

Is there a little bit of Sherlock Holmes or Harry Bosch in you? If so, consider the possibility of pursuing a career as a private detective or investigator. The work is not really very similar to the fiction you see in movies and television shows, but it can still be a challenge to courageous types.

Zeroing in on What a Private Detective or Investigator Does

Private detectives and investigators assist attorneys, government agencies, businesses, and the public with a variety of problems, such as tracing debtors, finding relatives or friends who have lost touch, or conducting background investigations. The main job of private investigators and some private detectives is to obtain information and locate assets or individuals. Some private detectives protect stores and hotels from theft, vandalism, and disorder.

Private detectives working as general investigators have duties ranging from locating missing persons to exposing fraudulent worker compensation claims. Some investigators specialize in one field, such as finance, where they might use accounting skills to investigate the financial standing of a company or locate funds stolen by an embezzler.

About half of all private investigators are self-employed or work for detective agencies. They specialize in missing persons, infidelity, and background investigations, including financial profiles and asset searches, physical surveillance, online computer database searches, and insurance investigations. They may obtain information, interview witnesses, and assemble evidence for litigation or criminal trials.

Many investigators spend considerable time conducting surveillance in the hope that they will observe inconsistencies in a subject's behavior. For example, a person who has recently filed a workers' compensation claim for an injury that has made walking difficult should not be able to jog or mow the lawn. If such behavior is observed, the investigator takes video or still photographs to document the activity and reports to the supervisor or client.

"Stakeouts" are a common form of surveillance. On a stakeout, an investigator regularly observes a site, such as the home of a subject, until the desired evidence is obtained. In an inconspicuous location, the investigator situates himself or herself and waits for information to emerge. Investigators are equipped with cameras (both still and video), binoculars, and citizen's band radios or car phones.

Some investigations involve verification of facts, such as an individual's place of employment or income. Thus, a phone call or visit to the workplace might be called for. In other investigations, especially in missing-person cases, the investigator interviews people to learn as much as possible about an individual's previous movements. These interviews can be formal or informal, friendly or confrontational.

Legal investigators specialize in cases involving the courts and lawyers. To assist in preparing criminal defenses, investigators locate witnesses, interview police, gather and review evidence, take photographs, and testify in court. To assist attorneys in the preparation of litigation for injured parties, they interview prospective witnesses, collect information on the parties involved in litigation, and search out testimonial, documentary, or physical evidence.

Corporate investigators work for companies other than investigative firms, often large corporations. In contrast to most private investigators, they report to a corporate chain of command. They conduct internal or external investigations. External investigations consist of preventing criminal schemes, thefts of company assets, and fraudulent deliveries of products by suppliers. With internal investigations, they prevent expense account abuse and catch employees who are stealing.

Investigators who specialize in finance may be hired to investigate the financial standing of companies or individuals. These investigators often work with investment bankers and lawyers. They generally develop confidential financial profiles of companies or individuals who may be parties to large financial transactions. An asset search is a common type of such an investigation.

Private detectives and investigators who work for large retail stores or malls are responsible for loss control and asset protection. Store detectives safeguard the assets of retail stores by apprehending persons attempting to steal merchandise or destroy store property. They detect theft by shoplifters, vendor representatives, delivery personnel, and even store employees. Store detectives also conduct periodic inspections of stock areas, dressing rooms, and rest rooms, and sometimes they assist in the opening and closing of the store. They may prepare loss-prevention and security reports for management and testify in court against persons they apprehend.

Computers have changed the nature of this profession and have become an integral part of investigative work. They allow investigators to obtain massive amounts of information in short periods of time from the dozens of online databases containing probate records, motor-vehicle registrations, credit reports, association membership lists, and other information.

Private investigators often work irregular hours, including mornings, evenings, weekends, and holidays. The irregular hours result from the need to conduct surveillance and contact people who may not be available during normal working hours. Insurance and corporate investigators have more normal work hours.

Many investigators spend much time away from their offices, conducting interviews or doing surveillance; others work in their offices most of the day, conducting computer searches and making phone calls. Corporate investigators often split their time between the office and the field; work done in the office generally consists of computer research. Store and hotel detectives work mostly in the businesses that they protect.

When away from the office, investigators spend time in environments that range from plush boardrooms to seedy bars. Investigators generally work alone, but sometimes they work with others during surveillance or stakeouts.

Some of the work that detectives and investigators do can be confrontational because the person being observed may not want to be observed. As a result, the job can be quite stressful and sometimes dangerous. Some investigators carry handguns, but most do not since it is difficult in many jurisdictions to obtain a permit to carry a concealed weapon. Owners of investigations firms have the added stress of having to deal with demanding and sometimes distraught clients.

Qualifications and Training Required for Private Detectives and Investigators

While there are no formal education requirements for most private detective and investigator jobs, many private detectives have college degrees. Almost all private detectives and investigators have previous experience in other occupations. Some work from the outset for insurance or collections companies or in the private security industry. Many investigators enter the field after serving in law enforcement, the military, government auditing and investigative positions, or federal intelligence jobs.

Former law enforcement officers, military investigators, and government agents often become private detectives or investigators as a second career because they are frequently able to retire after twenty years of service in the first career. Others enter from such diverse fields as finance, accounting, commercial credit, investigative reporting, insurance, and law. These individuals often can apply their prior work experience in a related investigative specialty. A few enter the occupation directly after graduation from college, generally with associate or bachelor of criminal justice or police science degrees.

The majority of states and the District of Columbia require private detectives and investigators to be licensed. Licensing requirements vary widely. Convicted felons cannot receive licenses in most states, and a number of states have enacted mandatory training programs for private detectives and investigators. Some states have relatively few requirements. Six states (Alabama, Alaska, Colorado, Idaho, Mississippi, and South Dakota) have no statewide licensing requirements, while others have stringent regulations. In California, for example, private investigators must be eighteen years of age or older; have a combination of education in police science, criminal law, or justice; have three years or six thousand hours of investigative experience; pass an evaluation by the U.S. Department of Justice and a criminal history background check; and receive a qualifying score on a two-hour written examination covering laws and regulations. There are additional requirements for firearms permits.

In considering candidates for private detective and investigator jobs, most employers look for individuals with ingenuity, persistence, and assertiveness. A candidate must not be afraid of confrontation, should communicate well, and should be able to think on his or her feet. Good interviewing and interrogation skills also are important and usually are acquired in earlier careers in law enforcement or other fields. Because the courts often are the ultimate judge of a properly conducted investigation, the investigator must be able to present the facts of a case in a manner a jury will believe.

Training in subjects such as criminal justice is helpful to aspiring private detectives and investigators. Most corporate investigators must have bachelor's degrees, preferably in a business-related field. Some corporate investigators have master's degrees in business administration or law, while others are certified public accountants. Corporate investigators hired by large companies may receive formal training from their employers on business practices, management structure, and various finance-related topics. The screening process for potential employees typically includes background checks of candidates' criminal history.

Some investigators receive certification from a professional organization to demonstrate competency in a field. For example, the National Association of Legal Investigators (NALI) confers the designation Certified Legal Investigator to licensed investigators who devote a majority of their practice to negligence or criminal defense investigations. To receive the designation, applicants must satisfy experience, education, and continuing training requirements and must pass written and oral exams administered by the NALI.

Most private detective agencies are small, with little room for advancement. Usually there are no defined ranks or steps, so advancement takes the form of increases in salary and assignment status. Many detectives and investigators work for detective agencies at the beginning of their careers and, after a few years, start their own firms. Corporate and legal investigators may rise to supervisory or managerial positions in the security or investigations department.

Job Settings for Private Detectives and Investigators

Private detectives and investigators held about thirty-nine thousand jobs in 2000. About two out of five were self-employed. Approximately a third of salaried private detectives and investigators worked for detective agencies, while another third were employed as store detectives in department or clothing and accessories stores. The remainder worked for hotels and other lodging places, legal services firms, and in other industries.

Salaries for Private Detectives and Investigators

According to the U.S. Department of Labor, median annual earnings of salaried private detectives and investigators were $26,750 in 2000. The middle 50 percent earned between $20,040 and $38,240. The lowest 10 percent earned less than $16,210, and the highest 10 percent earned more than $52,200. Median annual earnings were $21,180 in department stores, the industry employing the largest numbers of private detectives and investigators.

Salaries for private detectives and investigators vary greatly depending on the employer, specialty, and geographic area. According to a study by Abbott, Langer & Associates, security/loss-prevention directors and vice presidents had a median income of $77,500 per year in 2000; investigators, $39,800; and store detectives, $25,000. In addition to typical benefits, most corporate investigators received profit-sharing plans.

Job Outlook

In the near future, keen competition is expected in this field because private detective and investigator careers attract many qualified people, including relatively young retirees from law enforcement and military careers. Opportunities will be best for entry-level jobs with detective agencies or as part-time store detectives. Those seeking store detective jobs have the best prospects with large chains and discount stores.

Overall employment of private detectives and investigators is expected to grow faster than the average for all occupations through 2010. In addition to growth, replacement of those who retire or leave the occupation for other reasons should create many additional job openings. Increased demand for private detectives and investigators will result from fear of crime, increased litigation, and the need to protect confidential information and property of all kinds. More private investigators also will be needed to assist attorneys working on criminal defense and civil litigation.

Increasing financial activity worldwide will increase the demand for investigators to control internal and external financial losses and to monitor competitors and prevent industrial spying.

For Additional Information

Most states have associations for private detectives and investigators that provide career information. For information on local licensing requirements or other relevant information, contact your state police headquarters or state or provincial association or one of the organizations listed below.

Canadian Association for Security and Intelligence Studies
P.O. Box 69006
Place Ville Marie
Ottawa, ON K1R 1A7
Canada
www.casis.ca

Canadian Society for Industrial Security
141 Bentley Avenue, Unit B
Ottawa, ON K2E 6T7
Canada
www.csis-scsi.org

Criminal Defense Investigation Training Council
800 East Ocean Boulevard, Suite D
Stuart, FL 34994
www.defenseinvestigator.com

National Association of Legal Investigators
908 Twenty-First Street
Sacramento, CA 95814
www.nalionline.org

National Association of Professional Process Servers
P.O. Box 4547
Portland, OR 97208
www.napps.org

National Council of Investigation and Security Services
1730 M Street NW, Suite 200
Washington, DC 20036
www.nciss.org

Special Forces Officers

For a career that definitely requires courage, don't overlook the military. One example is the role of the special forces officer. Each branch of the military services (army, navy, air force, and marines) has specially trained forces to perform rapid-strike missions. These elite forces stay in a constant state of readiness to strike anywhere in the world on a moment's notice. Special forces officers lead special operations forces in offensive raids, demolitions, intelligence gathering, and search-and-rescue missions. Due to the wide variety of missions, special forces officers are trained swimmers, parachutists, and survival experts.

Zeroing in on What a Special Forces Officer Does

Special forces officers train personnel in parachute, scuba diving, and special combat techniques. They also plan missions and coordinate plans with other forces as needed; train personnel for special missions using simulated mission conditions; and lead special forces teams in accomplishing mission objectives. The latter may occur as peacetime training activities or may involve actual combat. In all recent wars and in special circumstances outside the bounds of declared wars, special forces have played key roles.

Qualifications and Training Required for Special Forces Officers

A bachelor's degree is normally required to qualify as a special forces officer, with helpful fields of study including physical education, engineering, physical sciences, history, and business or public administration. Helpful attributes include the ability to remain calm and decisive under stress, the determination to complete a very demanding training program, a willingness to accept challenges and face danger, and a willingness to stay in top physical condition.

In addition to previous military training, specific training for this role consists of up to twenty weeks of initial classroom training and practical experience. Training length varies depending on the specialty. Additional training occurs on the job. Basic skills are kept sharp through planning and conducting exercises under simulated mission conditions. Topics of study typically include physical conditioning, scuba diving, swimming, parachuting, mission planning techniques, handling and using explosives, and reconnaissance techniques.

Special forces officers must meet very demanding physical requirements. Good eyesight, night vision, and physical conditioning are required to reach mission objectives by parachute, over land, or underwater. Good hand-eye coordination is required to detonate or deactivate explosives. In most instances, special operations officers are required to be qualified swimmers, parachutists, and endurance runners.

Salaries for Special Forces Officers

The salaries earned by military personnel range from less than $12,000 per year to more than $130,000 annually, depending on factors such as years of experience and rank. Special forces officers tend to earn well above the minimum, since they are typically experienced personnel.

In addition to basic pay, military personnel receive free room and board (or a tax-free housing and subsistence allowance), medical and dental care, a military clothing allowance, military supermarket and department store shopping privileges, thirty days of paid vacation a year (referred to as leave), and travel opportunities. In many duty stations, military personnel may receive a housing allowance that can be used for off-base housing. This allowance can be substantial but varies greatly by rank and duty station. Other allowances are paid for foreign duty, hazardous duty, submarine and flight duty, and employment as a medical officer. Athletic and other facilities—such as gymnasiums, tennis courts, golf courses, bowling centers, libraries, and movie theaters—are available on many military installations. Military personnel are eligible for retirement benefits after twenty years of service.

The Veterans Administration (VA) provides numerous benefits to those who have served at least two years in the armed forces. Veterans are eligible for free care in VA hospitals for all service-related disabilities. Those with other medical problems are eligible for free VA care if they are unable to pay the cost of hospitalization elsewhere. Admission to a VA medical center depends on the availability of beds, however. Veterans also are eligible for certain loans, including home loans. Veterans, regardless of health, can convert a military life insurance policy to an individual policy with any participating company in the veteran's state of residence. In addition, job counseling, testing, and placement services are available. Veterans who participate in the Montgomery GI Bill Program receive educational benefits.

Job Settings for Special Forces Officers

Because special forces officers must be prepared to go anywhere in the world they are needed, they train and work in all climates, weather conditions, and settings. They may work in cold water and dive from submarines or small underwater craft. They may also be exposed to harsh temperatures, often without protection, during missions into enemy-controlled areas.

Related Opportunities

Although the job of special forces officer has no equivalent in civilian life, the leadership and administrative skills it provides are similar to those used in many civilian management occupations, particularly law enforcement.

The services normally have about twenty-five hundred special forces officers. Each year, they need new special forces officers due to changes in personnel and the demands of the field. After training, special forces officers usually assist commanders in directing special operations forces. After demonstrating leadership ability, they may assume command positions.

Other military roles provide opportunities for courageous types. They include a wide variety of positions in the army, navy, air force, marines, and coast guard.

For Additional Information

Military Advantage, Inc.
544 Pacific Avenue, Suite 300
San Francisco, CA 94133
www.military.com

Military Careers
Defense Manpower Data Center
DoD Center–Monterey Bay
400 Gigling Road
Seaside, CA 93955
www.careersinthemilitary.com

Today's Military
www.todaysmilitary.com

. . . .

Pilots

Although the previously described role of test pilot may be especially challenging, the work performed by other types of aircraft pilots can also be highly appealing to courageous types. Here is a look at the exciting work done by today's pilots.

The pilots of the twenty-first century are highly trained professionals who fly airplanes or helicopters to carry out a wide variety of tasks. Although the majority are airline pilots, copilots, and flight engineers who transport passengers and cargo, others are commercial pilots involved in more unusual tasks. Their work may include dusting crops, spreading seed for reforestation, flying passengers and cargo to areas not serviced by regular airlines, directing fire fighting efforts, tracking criminals, monitoring traffic, and rescuing and evacuating injured persons.

Zeroing in on What Pilots Do

Except on small aircraft, two pilots usually make up the cockpit crew for any airplane. Generally, the most experienced pilot, the captain, is in command and supervises all other crew members. The pilot and copilot share flying and other duties, such as communicating with air traffic controllers and monitoring the instruments. Some large aircraft have a third pilot—the flight engineer—who assists the other pilots by monitoring and operating many of the instruments and systems, making minor in-flight repairs, and watching for other aircraft. New technology can perform many flight tasks, however, and virtually all new aircraft now fly with only two pilots, who rely more heavily on computerized controls. As older, less technologically sophisticated aircraft continue to be retired from airline fleets, the number of flight engineer jobs is expected to decrease.

Pilots plan their flights carefully before making them. They thoroughly check their aircraft to make sure that the engines, controls, instruments, and other systems are functioning properly. They also make sure that baggage or cargo has been loaded correctly. Pilots confer with flight dispatchers and aviation weather forecasters to find out about weather conditions en route and at the destination. Based on this information, they choose the route, altitude, and speed that will provide the fastest, safest, and smoothest flight. When flying under instrument flight rules (procedures governing the operation of the aircraft when there is poor visibility) the pilot in command, or the company dispatcher, normally files an instrument flight plan with air traffic control so that the flight can be coordinated with other air traffic.

The most challenging parts of any flight typically occur during takeoffs and landings, demanding close coordination between the pilot and first officer. As the plane accelerates for takeoff, for example, the pilot concentrates on the runway while the first officer scans the instrument panel. To calculate the speed they must attain to become airborne, pilots consider the altitude of the airport, outside temperature, weight of the plane, and speed and direction of the wind. The moment the plane reaches takeoff speed, the first officer informs the pilot, who then pulls back on the controls to raise the nose of the plane.

If the weather is good, most flights are relatively easy. Airplane pilots, with the assistance of autopilot and the flight management computer, steer the plane along the planned route and are monitored by the air traffic control stations they pass along the way. They regularly scan the instrument panel to check the fuel supply, the condition of the engines, and the air-conditioning, hydraulic, and other systems.

Pilots may request a change in altitude or route if circumstances dictate. For instance, if the ride is rougher than expected, they may ask air traffic control if pilots flying at other altitudes have reported better conditions. If so, they may request an altitude change. This procedure also may be used to find a stronger tailwind or a weaker head wind to save fuel and increase speed.

Unlike most airplanes, helicopters are used for short trips at relatively low altitude, so pilots must be constantly on the lookout for trees, bridges, power lines, transmission towers, and other dangerous obstacles. Regardless of the type of aircraft, all pilots must monitor warning devices designed to help detect sudden shifts in wind conditions that can cause crashes.

When visibility is poor, pilots must rely completely on their instruments. On the basis of altimeter readings, they know how high above ground they are and whether they can fly safely over mountains and other obstacles. Special navigation radios give pilots precise information that, with the help of special maps, tells them their exact position. Other very sophisticated equipment provides directions to a point just above the end of a runway and enables pilots to land completely "blind." Once on the ground, pilots must complete records on the flight for the organization as well as for the FAA report.

Most pilots also have some nonflying duties. Although airline pilots have the services of large support staffs and thus perform relatively few nonflying tasks, those employed by other organizations, such as charter operators or businesses, have many other duties. They may load the aircraft, handle all passenger luggage to ensure a balanced load, and supervise refueling. Other nonflying responsibilities may include keeping records, scheduling flights, arranging for major maintenance, and performing minor aircraft maintenance and repair work.

Some pilots also serve as instructors. They teach their students the principles of flight in ground-school classes and demonstrate how to operate aircraft in dual-controlled planes and helicopters. A few specially trained pilots are "examiners" or "check pilots." They periodically fly with other pilots or pilot's license applicants to make sure that they are proficient.

Job Settings for Pilots

Although flying does not involve unusual physical effort, the mental stress of being responsible for a safe flight, no matter what the weather, can be tiring. Pilots must be alert and quick to react if something goes wrong, particularly during takeoff and landing.

By law, airline pilots cannot fly more than one hundred hours a month or more than one thousand hours a year. Most airline pilots fly an average of seventy-five hours a month and work an additional seventy-five hours a month performing nonflying duties.

About one-fourth of all pilots work more than forty hours a week. Most spend a considerable amount of time away from home because the majority of flights involve overnight layovers. When pilots are away from home, the airlines provide hotel accommodations, transportation between the hotel and airport, and an allowance for meals and other expenses. Airlines operate flights at all hours of the day and night, so work schedules often are irregular. Flight assignments are based on seniority.

Those pilots not employed by the airlines often have irregular schedules as well; they may fly thirty hours one month and ninety hours the next. Because these pilots frequently have many nonflying responsibilities, they have much less free time than do airline pilots. Except for business pilots, most do not remain away from home overnight. They may work odd hours. Flight instructors may have irregular and seasonal work schedules, depending on their students' available time and the weather. Instructors frequently work at night or on weekends.

Airline pilots, especially those on international routes, often suffer jet lag—fatigue caused by many hours of flying through different time zones. To guard against excessive pilot fatigue that could result in unsafe flying conditions, the FAA requires airlines to allow pilots at least eight hours of uninterrupted rest in the twenty-four hours before finishing their flight duty.

Some element of danger is involved in any type of flying, although great efforts are taken to assure the safety of air crews and passengers. In addition, pilots who are crop dusters may be exposed to toxic chemicals and seldom have the benefit of a regular landing strip. Helicopter pilots involved in police work may also be subject to personal injury.

Qualifications and Training Required for Pilots

All professional pilots must have a commercial pilot's license with an instrument rating issued by the Federal Aviation Administration (FAA). Helicopter pilots must hold a commercial pilot's certificate with a helicopter rating. To qualify for these licenses, applicants must be at least eighteen years old and have at least 250 hours of flight experience. The experience required can be reduced through participation in certain flight school curricula approved by the FAA.

Potential pilots must also pass a strict physical examination to make sure that they are in good health and have 20/20 vision (with or without glasses), good hearing, and no physical handicaps that could impair their performance. They must pass a written test that includes questions on the principles of safe flight, navigation techniques, and FAA regulations, and they must demonstrate their flying ability to FAA or designated examiners.

To fly in periods of low visibility, pilots must be rated by the FAA to fly by instruments. Pilots may qualify for this rating by having 105 hours of flight experience, including 40 hours of experience in flying by instruments; they also must pass a written examination on procedures and FAA regulations covering instrument flying; and they must demonstrate to an examiner their ability to fly by instruments.

Airline pilots must fulfill additional requirements. Pilots must have an airline transport pilot's license. Applicants for this license must be at least twenty-three years old and have a minimum of fifteen hundred hours of flying experience, including night and instrument flying, and must pass FAA written and flight examinations. Usually, they also have one or more advanced ratings, such as multiengine aircraft or aircraft type ratings dependent upon the requirements of their particular flying jobs. Because pilots must be able to make quick decisions and accurate judgments under pressure, many airline companies reject applicants who do not pass required psychological and aptitude tests. All licenses are valid as long as a pilot can pass the periodic physical examinations and tests of flying skills required by federal government and company regulations.

The armed forces have always been an important source of trained pilots for civilian jobs. Military pilots gain valuable experience on jet aircraft and helicopters, and persons with this experience usually are preferred for civilian pilot jobs. This primarily reflects the extensive flying time military pilots receive. Persons without armed forces training may become pilots by attending flight schools.

The FAA has certified about six hundred civilian flying schools, including some colleges and universities that offer degree credit for pilot training. Prospective pilots also may learn to fly by taking lessons from individual FAA-certified flight instructors.

While some small airlines will hire high school graduates, most airlines require at least two years of college and prefer to hire college graduates. Because the number of college-educated applicants continues to increase, many employers are making a college degree the basic educational requirement.

New airline pilots start as first officers or flight engineers. Although some airlines favor applicants who already have a flight engineer's license, they may provide flight engineer training for those who have only the commercial license. Many pilots begin with smaller regional or commuter airlines, where they obtain experience flying passengers on scheduled flights into busy airports in all weather conditions. These jobs often lead to higher-paying jobs with larger national airlines.

Training for new airline pilots includes a week of company orientation, three to six weeks of ground school and simulator training, and twenty-five hours of initial operating experience, including a check ride with an FAA aviation safety inspector. Experienced pilots are required to attend recurrent training and simulator checks twice a year throughout their careers.

Employers other than airlines usually require less flying experience. A commercial pilot's license is a minimum requirement, and employers tend to prefer applicants who have experience in the type of craft they will be flying. New employees usually start as first officers or fly less-sophisticated equipment.

Advancement for all pilots usually is limited to other flying jobs. Many pilots start as flight instructors, building their flying hours while they earn money teaching. As they become more experienced, these pilots occasionally fly charter planes or perhaps get jobs with small air transportation firms, such as air taxi companies. Some advance to business flying jobs. A small number get flight engineer jobs with the airlines.

Career advancement for airline pilots usually depends on the seniority provisions of union contracts. After one to five years, flight engineers advance according to seniority to first officer and then, after five to fifteen years, to captain. Seniority also determines which pilots get the more desirable routes. Outside of the airline industry, a first officer may advance to pilot and, in large companies, to chief pilot or director of aviation in charge of aircraft scheduling, maintenance, and flight procedures.

Salaries of Pilots

Aircraft pilots and flight engineers earn salaries that vary greatly depending whether they work as airline or commercial pilots.

Earnings of airline pilots are among the highest in the nation and depend on factors such as the type, size, and maximum speed of the plane and the number of hours and miles flown. For example, pilots who fly jet aircraft usually earn higher salaries than do pilots who fly turboprops.

Airline pilots and flight engineers may also earn extra pay for night and international flights.

In 2000, median annual earnings of airline pilots, copilots, and flight engineers were $110,940, according to the U.S. Department of Labor. The lowest 10 percent earned less than $36,110. Over 25 percent earned more than $145,000.

Median annual earnings of commercial pilots were $43,300 in 2000. The middle 50 percent earned between $31,500 and $61,230. The lowest 10 percent earned less than $24,290, and the highest 10 percent earned more than $92,000.

Airline pilots usually are eligible for life and health insurance plans financed by the airlines. They also receive retirement benefits and, if they fail the FAA physical examination at some point in their careers, they get disability payments. In addition, pilots receive an expense allowance, or per diem, for time spent away from home.

Some airlines also provide allowances to pilots for purchasing and cleaning their uniforms. As an additional benefit, pilots and their immediate families may be entitled to free or reduced fare transportation on their own and other airlines.

More than half of all aircraft pilots are members of unions. Most of the pilots who fly for the major airlines are members of the Air Line Pilots Association, International.

For Additional Information

The Air Line Pilots Association
535 Herndon Parkway
Herndon, VA 20170
www.alpa.org

Air Transport Association (ATA)
1301 Pennsylvania Avenue NW, Suite 1100
Washington, DC 20004
www.airlines.org

Coalition of Airline Pilots Associations (CAPA)
1101 Pennsylvania Avenue NW, Suite 6646
Washington, DC 20004
www.capapilots.org

Federal Aviation Administration (FAA)
800 Independence Avenue SW
Washington, DC 20591
www.faa.gov

Independent Pilots Association (IPA)
3607 Fern Valley Road
Louisville, KY 40219
www.ipapilot.org

National EMS Pilots Association (NEMSPA)
526 King Street, Suite 415
Alexandria, VA 22314
www.nemspa.org

National Pilots Association (NPA)
ATL Air Center, Suite 275
3401 Norman Berry Drive
Atlanta, GA 30344
www.npa-atl.org

Professional Helicopter Pilots Association (PHPA)
1809 Clearview Parkway, Suite A
Metairie, LA 70001
www.autorotate.org

Ship's Captains or Crew Members

For many, working on the high seas (or other bodies of water) can form the basis of an adventurous career. For example, captains, mates, and pilots command or supervise the operations of ships and other water vessels. For captains or masters, this role means being in overall command of the operation of a vessel. Common tasks include supervising other officers and crew members, determining course and speed, and monitoring the vessel's position using charts and navigational aides. They also oversee the work of others in areas such as navigation, communications, engine operations, and maintenance.

Zeroing in on What a Ship's Captain or Crew Member Does

Ship's officers and other crew members move huge amounts of cargo and passengers between nations as well as domestically. They operate and maintain deep-sea merchant ships, tugboats, towboats, ferries, dredges, excursion vessels, and other waterborne craft in the oceans, the Great Lakes, rivers, harbors, canals, and other waterways.

The captain's role is an elite one, at least on some types of ships, and that in itself carries a certain amount of glamour. On top of that, the excitement of traveling from one destination to another can be rewarding for the right type of personality.

Certainly only a relative few can operate at the top level, but related jobs can also appeal to courageous types. Deck officers or mates, for example, perform the work for captains on vessels when they are on watch. Mates also supervise and coordinate activities of the crew aboard the ship. They inspect the cargo holds during loading to ensure the load is stowed according to specifications and regulations.

A major responsibility for mates is supervising crew members engaged in maintenance and the primary upkeep of the vessel. Mates stand watch for specified periods, usually four hours on and eight hours off. However, on smaller vessels, there may be only one mate (called a pilot on some inland towing vessels), who alternates watches with the captain. The mate would assume command of the ship if the captain became incapacitated. When more than one mate is necessary aboard a ship, they typically are designated chief mate or first mate, second mate, and third mate.

Pilots play a different role. They guide ships in and out of harbors, through straits, and on rivers and other confined waterways where a familiarity with local water depths, winds, tides, currents, and hazards such as reefs and shoals are of prime importance. Pilots on river and canal vessels are usually regular crew members, like mates. Harbor pilots, who are generally independent contractors, accompany vessels while they enter or leave port. They may pilot many ships in a single day. Motorboat operators run small, motor-driven boats to carry passengers and freight. They also take depth soundings in turning basins and serve as liaisons between ships or between ship and shore, harbor and beach, or area patrols.

Of interest to mechanical as well as courageous types is the work of ship engineers. They operate, maintain, and repair propulsion engines, boilers, generators, pumps, and other machinery. Merchant marine vessels usually have four engineering officers: a chief engineer and first, second, and third assistant engineers. Assistant engineers stand periodic watches, overseeing the safe operation of engines and machinery.

Marine oilers and more experienced qualified members of the engine department, or QMEDs, maintain the proper running order of their vessels in the engine spaces below decks under the direction of the ship's engineering officers. They lubricate gears, shafts, bearings, and other moving parts of engines and motors; read pressure and temperature gauges and record data; and may assist with repairs and adjust machinery.

What about sailors? They operate the vessel and its deck equipment under the direction of the ship's officers and keep the nonengineering areas in good condition. Sailors stand watch, looking out for other vessels and obstructions in the ship's path and navigational aids such as buoys and lighthouses. They also steer the ship, measure water depth in shallow water, and maintain and operate deck equipment such as lifeboats, anchors, and cargo-handling gear. On vessels handling liquid cargo, sailors hook up hoses, operate pumps, and clean tanks. On tugboats or tow vessels, they tie barges together into tow units, inspect them periodically, and disconnect them when the destination is reached.

When docking or departing, sailors handle lines. They also perform routine maintenance chores such as repairing lines, chipping rust, and painting and cleaning decks or other areas. Experienced sailors are designated able seamen on ocean-going vessels, but they may just be called deckhands on inland waters; larger vessels usually have a boatswain, or head seaman.

A typical deep-sea merchant ship has a captain, three deck officers or mates, a chief engineer and three assistant engineers, a radio operator, plus six or more nonofficers, such as deck seamen, oilers and QMEDs, and cooks or food handlers. The size and service of the ship determine the number of crew for a particular voyage. Small vessels operating in harbors, rivers, or along the coast may have a crew comprised only of a captain and one deckhand. Cooking responsibilities usually fall under the deckhand's duties.

Crews on larger coastal ships may include a captain, a mate or pilot, an engineer, and seven or eight seamen. Nonlicensed positions on a large ship may include a full-time cook, an electrician, and machinery mechanics. On cruise ships, which also may be considered coastal ships, bedroom stewards keep passengers' quarters clean and comfortable.

Job Settings for Ship's Captains and Crew Members

Working environments vary widely in this occupational area. Merchant mariners, for example, spend extended periods at sea. Most deep-sea mariners are hired for one or more voyages that last for several months, although there is no job security after that voyage. Many are unemployed for weeks or months before they have another opportunity to join another ship's crew.

The rate of unionization for these workers is much higher than the average for all occupations. Most merchant marine officers and seamen, both veterans and beginners, are hired for voyages through union hiring halls or directly by shipping companies. Hiring halls prioritize the candidates by the length of time the person has been out of work and fill open slots accordingly. Hiring halls are typically found in major seaports.

While at sea, these workers usually stand watch for four hours and are off for eight hours, seven days a week. Those employed on Great Lakes ships typically work sixty days and have thirty days off, but they do not work in the winter, when the lakes are frozen.

Workers on rivers, canals, and in harbors are more likely to have year-round work. Some work eight- or twelve-hour shifts and go home every day. Others work steadily for a week or a month and then have an extended period off. When working, they are usually on duty for six or twelve hours and then are off for six or twelve hours. Those on smaller vessels are normally assigned to one vessel and have steady employment.

The officers and crews of ships work in all weather conditions. Although merchant mariners try to avoid severe storms while at sea, working in damp and cold conditions is often inevitable. It is uncommon nowadays for vessels to suffer sea disasters such as fire, explosion, or sinking, but workers do face the possibility that they may have to abandon ship on short notice if it collides with other vessels or runs aground. They also risk injury or death from falling overboard as well as hazards associated with working with machinery, heavy loads, and dangerous cargo.

Most newer vessels are air-conditioned, soundproofed from noisy machinery, and equipped with comfortable living quarters. Nevertheless, some mariners dislike the long periods away from home and the confinement aboard ship and consequently leave the industry.

Qualifications and Training Required for Ship's Captains and Crew Members

Employees in this area must meet entry, training, and educational requirements established and regulated by the U.S. Coast Guard, an agency of the U.S. Department of Transportation. All officers and operators of watercraft must be licensed by the coast guard, which offers various kinds of licenses, depending on the position and type of craft.

To qualify for a deck or engineering officer's license, applicants must either accumulate sea time and meet regulatory requirements or must graduate from the U.S. Merchant Marine Academy or one of the six state maritime academies. In both cases, applicants must pass a written examination. Federal regulations also require that an applicant pass a physical examination, a drug screening, and a National Driver Register Check before being considered.

Men and women without formal training can be licensed if they pass the written exam and possess sea service appropriate to the license for which they are applying. However, it is difficult to pass the examination without substantial formal schooling or independent study, according to the U.S. Department of Transportation. Also, because sailors may work six months a year or less, it can take five to eight years to accumulate the necessary experience.

The academies offer a four-year academic program leading to a bachelor of science degree, a license as a third mate (deck officer) or third assistant engineer (engineering officer) issued by the coast guard, and, if the person is qualified, a commission as ensign in the U.S. Naval Reserve, Merchant Marine Reserve, or the Coast Guard Reserve. With experience and additional training, third officers may qualify for higher rank.

Sailors and unlicensed engineers working on U.S. flagged deep-sea and Great Lakes vessels must hold a coast guard–issued document. They must also hold certification when working aboard liquid-carrying vessels. Able seamen must hold government-issued certification. For employment in the merchant marine as an unlicensed seaman, a merchant mariner's document issued by the coast guard is needed.

A medical certificate of excellent health attesting to vision, color perception, and general physical condition is required for higher-level deckhands and unlicensed engineers. While no experience or formal schooling is required, training at a union-operated school is the best source. Beginners are classified as ordinary seamen and may be assigned to any of the three unlicensed departments: deck, engine, or steward. With experience at sea, and perhaps union-sponsored training, an ordinary seaman can pass the able seaman exam and move up after three years of service.

No special training or experience is needed to become a seaman or deckhand on vessels operating in harbors or on rivers or other waterways. Newly hired workers are generally given a short intro-ductory course and then learn skills on the job. After sufficient experience, they are eligible to take a coast guard exam to qualify as a mate, pilot, or captain. Substantial knowledge gained through experience, courses taught at approved schools, and independent study are needed to pass the exam.

Harbor pilot training is usually an extended apprenticeship with a towing company or a pilot association. Entrants may be able seamen or licensed officers.

Salaries of Ship's Officers and Crew

There is a wide range of salaries in this area. Wages may vary from minimum wage for some beginning seamen or mate positions to more than $33 an hour for some experienced ship engineers.

According to the U.S. Department of Labor, median hourly earnings for ship and boat captains and operators were $21.62 in 2000. The median for ship engineers was $22.85 per hour, and for sailors and marine oilers it was $13.52

For captains of larger vessels, such as container ships, oil tankers, or passenger ships, annual earnings may exceed $100,000, but only after many years of experience.

For Additional Information

International Organization of Masters, Mates, and Pilots
700 Maritime Boulevard
Linthicum Heights, MD 21090
www.bridgedeck.com

Maritime Administration
U.S. Department of Transportation
400 Seventh Street SW
Washington, DC 20590
www.marad.dot.gov

Paul Hall Center for Maritime Training and Education
P.O. Box 75
Piney Point, MD 20674
www.seafarers.org/phc

Seafarers International Union
5201 Auth Way
Camp Springs, MD 20746
www.seafarers.org

U.S. Coast Guard Recruiting
4200 Wilson Boulevard, Suite 450
Arlington, VA 22203
www.uscg.mil

U.S. Merchant Marine Academy
300 Steamboat Road
Kings Point, NY 11024
www.usmma.edu

For Further Reading

Adams, Bob, and Laura Morin. *The Complete Resume and Job Search Book for College Students*. Adams Media Corporation, 1999.

Bloch, Deborah Perlmutter. *How to Get Your First Job and Keep It*. McGraw-Hill, 2002.

Bolles, Richard Nelson. *What Color Is Your Parachute 2004: A Practical Manual for Job-Hunters and Career Changers*. Ten Speed Press, 2003.

Cunningham, John R. *The Inside Scoop: Recruiters Share Their Tips on Job Search Success with College Students*. McGraw-Hill, 2001.

Deluca, Matthew J. *Best Answers to the 201 Most Frequently Asked Interview Questions*. McGraw-Hill, 1996.

Deluca, Matthew, and Nanette Deluca. *More Best Answers to the 201 Most Frequently Asked Interview Questions*. McGraw-Hill, 2001.

Drake, John D. *The Perfect Interview: How to Get the Job You Really Want*. Fine Publications, 2002.

Eisenberg, Ronni. *Organize Your Job Search!* Hyperion Press, 2000.

Jansen, Julie. *I Don't Know What I Want, but I Know It's Not This: A Step-By-Step Guide to Finding Gratifying Work*. Penguin USA, 2003.

Gale, Linda, and Barry Gale. *Discover What You're Best At: A Complete Career System That Lets You Test Yourself to Discover Your Own True Career Abilities*. Simon and Schuster, 1998.

Garber, Janet. *Getting a Job*. Silver Lining Books, 2003.

Gisler, Margaret, and Jamie Miller. *101 Career Alternatives for Teachers: Exciting Job Opportunities for Teachers Outside the Teaching Profession*. Crown Publishing Group, 2002.

Graber, Steven, and Barry Littmann. *Everything Online Job Search Book: Find the Jobs, Send Your Resume and Land the Career of Your Dreams—All Online!* Adams Media Corporation, 2000.

Greene, Susan D., and Melanie C. Martel. *The Ultimate Job Hunter's Guidebook*. Houghton Mifflin Company, 2000.

Griffiths, Bob. *Do What You Love for the Rest of Your Life: A Practical Guide to Career Change and Personal Renewal*. Random House, 2001.

Masi, Mary, and Lauren B. Starkey. *Firefighter Career Starter*. LearningExpress, 2001.

McKinney, Anne, Editor. *Real Resumes for Career Changers: Actual Resumes and Cover Letters*. PREP Publishing, 2000.

O'Neill, Lucy. *Job Smarts*. Scholastic Library Publishing, 2001.

Resumes for First-Time Job Hunters. McGraw-Hill, 2000.

Shar, Barbara, and Barbara Smith. *I Could Do Anything if I Only Knew What It Was: How to Discover What You Really Want and How to Get It*. Dell Publishing, 1995.

Tieger, Paul, and Barbara Barron-Tieger. *Do What You Are: Discover the Perfect Career for You Through the Secrets of Personality Type*. Little, Brown and Company, 2001.

Whitcomb, Susan Britton, and Pat Kendall. *E-Resumes: Everything You Need to Know About Using Electronic Resumes to Tap into Today's Hot Job Market*. McGraw-Hill, 2001.

About the Author

J an Goldberg's love for the printed page began well before her second birthday. Regular visits to the book bindery where her grandfather worked produced a magical combination of sights and smells that she carries with her to this day.

Childhood was filled with composing poems and stories, reading books, and playing library. Elementary and high school included an assortment of contributions to school newspapers. While a full-time college student, Goldberg wrote extensively as part of her job responsibilities in the College of Business Administration at Roosevelt University in Chicago. After receiving a degree in elementary education, she was able to extend her love of reading and writing to her students.

Goldberg has written extensively in the occupations area for General Learning Corporation's *Career World Magazine* as well as for the many career publications produced by CASS Recruitment Publications. She has also contributed to a number of projects for educational publishers, including Scott Foresman and Addison-Wesley.

As a feature writer, Goldberg's work has appeared in *Parenting Magazine*, *Today's Chicago Woman*, *Opportunity Magazine*, *Chicago Parent*, *Complete Woman*, *North Shore Magazine*, and Pioneer Press newspapers. In all, she has published more than 250 pieces as a full-time freelance writer.

In addition to *Careers for Courageous People*, the other books she has written for VGM Career Books include: *On the Job: Real People Working in Communications*, *Great Jobs for Music Majors*,

Great Jobs for Computer Science Majors, Careers in Journalism, Opportunities in Research and Development Careers, and *Opportunities in Horticulture Careers.*

This edition of *Careers for Courageous People* was revised by Mark Rowh, a professional writer and the author of a number of other books published by McGraw-Hill.